Dedication

This book is dedicated to all of those at Howard Publishing who have worked so hard to bless my life. To Alton Howard and Gary Meyers who first approached me about working with them, and motivated me to finish projects that I would not have without them. To Philis Boultinghouse who worked tirelessly, and often with little gratitude, to edit my books and helped me to be a better writer. To John Howard who had faith in my writing and who has invested himself and his resources in order to make my books available to a much wider audience than I ever dreamed possible.

It is dedicated to my wife Judi – who deserves more credit than I do for the writing of this book, who for thirty-nine years has consistently given up everything she wanted for the sake of what I wanted. Who for thirty-nine years has been patient with my frustration – encouraging when I was down, thoughtful when I was tired, inspiring when I was defeated, understanding when I was discouraged, and kind when I was unkind. She has been my "angel" for thirty-nine years – and without her, this book would never have been written.

It is dedicated to the God of the heavens and the earth under whose grace and providential care I have lived since the day I was born. To His Son, Jesus the Christ whose life, and death and teachings have been the inspiration and guiding star of my life, And to the innumerable hosts of angels who have "ministered to me" most of my life, without my knowledge or appreciation.

It is gratefully dedicated to all of those who have made me believe that my writings have made a difference in their life.

John W. Smith

Table of Contents

What I want to do in this book
is not so much to "explain" prayer,
providence, or angels, or even to
help you to "understand" them —
no — what I want most to do
is to cause you to "wonder" about
them, and "believe" in them.

Introduction

This is a book about angels, about prayer, about the providence of God – and if you're interested in – "that sort of thing" – I think you'll really enjoy this book and it will bless your life. If you're not interested in – "that sort of thing" – you probably need to read this book more than those who are. What I want to do in this book is not so much to "explain" prayer, providence, or angels, or even to help you to "understand" them – no – what I want most to do is to cause you to "wonder" about them, and "believe" in them.

Perhaps I need at the very outset to tell you that this is not one of those, "who done it," type of science fiction, situation comedy novels about angels and demons that are so prevalent today. I mean those *National Enquirer* type of pulp novels, with soap opera plots, that pit slightly superhuman angels in white hats against slightly superhuman angels in black hats.

This book will not seek to play on your credulity and titillate your "dark side" curiosity by talking about angels who are simply the products of money minded marketing moguls. Those "pseudo angels" can do nice things for you, but they are so flawed, ridiculous, and tragic that although they may appeal to what is materialistic in us – they certainly do not call us to a greater faith in God's providence or encourage us to pray more. They are so woefully human, painfully obvious and pathetic that I think they actually keep us from recognizing the authentic angelic beings that God sends to us.

I do not deny that the "angels" depicted in those books – and the junior high plots they engage in – may be entertaining, but certainly no Biblically knowledgeable person would ever believe in them, or take them seriously. They do nothing to call us higher or closer to the spiritual realm. Rather they cause us to focus more on this material world – this world that is "passing away" – because that seems to be their only concern.

I want also to say that there are several subtle dangers in that kind of writing. One of them is that we may start believing that Satan and his angels are really that laughably weak – and simple minded – and that their plots for our destruction are so blatantly obvious; and so easily avoided that we need not take them seriously. We may forget that Satan is not only "real" – he is far more dangerous and deceptive than we ever imagined.

Often, when I read a book that really intrigues me, one of the first questions I ask is, "I wonder where the author got the idea for this book?" What I mean is, because I write books, I know that often the "inspiration" – the idea for a book is more difficult to come by than actually writing the book. I also know – because I am a writer – that often it is hard to pin down the exact source for an idea, and sometimes the author himself may not know where the idea came from, but in this case I do, and so I'm going to tell you.

Assembly of Angels

When I was preaching in San Diego, California – one Sunday I preached a sermon on a passage from Hebrews twelve, where there is a graphic description of the terrifying plight of the nation of Israel as they approached God at the foot of Mount Sinai while Moses went up to receive the law. The author compares Israel's reaction to that situation, with the reaction of Christians, as they approach God through the cross and the church, he gives us this inspiring and reassuring affirmation,

> *You* [Christians] have not come to a mountain that can be touched and that is burning with fire; to darkness, gloom and

storm; to a trumpet blast or to such a voice speaking words that those who heard it begged that no further word be spoken to them, because they could not bear what was commanded: "If even an animal touches the mountain, it must be stoned." The sight was so terrifying that Moses said, "I am trembling with fear." But *you* have come to Mount Zion, to the heavenly Jerusalem, the city of the living God. *You have come to thousands upon thousands of angels in joyful assembly*, to the church of the firstborn, whose names are written in heaven. You have come to God, the judge of all men, to the spirits of righteous men made perfect, to Jesus the mediator of a new covenant, and to the sprinkled blood that speaks a better word than the blood of Abel.

After the sermon I was standing at the door greeting my parishioners, and Kwaku Dayie – a young man from Ghana who is a postdoctoral research scientist at the Scripps Institute and one of my more thoughtful and spiritual members – told me that he had never noticed that reference to Christians coming to "thousands upon thousands of angels in joyful assembly" before. He said that he had never *experienced* that, and he wondered if I ever had. When I hesitantly said, "no, I don't think I have," he asked why that might be true, and what I thought that it meant. My first reaction was panic, because I didn't have a clue, and the "preacher" is always supposed to know. I made some lame comment about needing more time than I had at the moment to explain it, and excused myself as another parishioner came up to greet me.

But Kwaku's question stayed with me, and on Monday, as I went back over the sermon, I realized that not only did I not have a clue, what was much more disturbing – I had never even thought about it.

I got to thinking about why a person who normally has a very imaginative and inquisitive mind had never paid any attention to such powerful and visionary imagery before. I thought maybe it was time I did.

I started by looking up all the Bible passages about angels that I could find, and I was astonished first, to find that there are so many of them, and second, to find them so *graphic* – and strangely enough at the same time – so *matter of fact*. And it occurred to me that maybe the reason I hadn't thought too much about them was because they are so *matter of fact*.

What I mean by, "matter of fact," is that the Bible doesn't present a long exegetical explanation of the "angel phenomenon," or try to "prove" that there are angels, or that angels are, "perfectly reasonable," any more than it tries to "prove" that it is "perfectly reasonable" to believe in God – it just "assumes" them. The Bible also doesn't try to draw attention to angels by making a big deal out of them – it just sort of "slips them in" as part of the story. Sometimes their role is so unobtrusive that we don't even notice they're there. Let me give you some examples.

Hagar and Ishmael

In Genesis 21, beginning at verse 14: Moses is relating the story of Abraham, Sarah, Isaac, Hagar and Ishmael. At some point after Sarah gives birth to Isaac, she decides that she doesn't want him raised with Ishmael, and so she insists that Abraham send Hagar and Ishmael away. Moses says,

> Early the next morning Abraham took some food and a skin of water and gave them to Hagar. He set them on her shoulders and then sent her off with the boy. She went on her way and wandered in the desert of Beersheba. When the water in the skin was gone, she put him under one of the bush-

been wearing any socks it would have) because they probably thought he was coming after them. But they have this job to do and they pull out their swords and get ready to defend themselves.

But the angel doesn't pay any attention to them, he just walks over to the tomb and shoves aside this huge rock blocking the entrance (how do I know it was huge – I'll tell you why – because people can walk in and out of this tomb, which means that it had a very large entrance, and you can't block up a hole that size with a pebble. Besides, after the angel shoved the rock aside he "sat down" on it – that's how.) Anyway, he pushes this huge rock that is blocking the entrance to one side – (which means that angels are very strong) – and he sits down on it. And says to these Roman soldiers, "Well, what are you going to do about that – I don't think you want to mess with me, because I will take those silly swords of yours and shove them up your nose." And I don't blame those soldiers for passing out cold.

The Bible says that the angel's appearance was, "like lightning." What does that mean? At first I assumed that it meant that he came real fast, as in that graphic phrase we use – "like greased lightning," but then I thought maybe it meant that he "looked" like lightning – which I suppose means that he was all forked and jagged and bright, and you have to admit that would be something to see. But this angel was "dressed," he had these extremely white clothes on, and I wondered what kind of clothes you would put on a lightning bolt – they must have been made out of asbestos, but that couldn't be true, because if his clothes were made of asbestos – he might have died of cancer – and what's even worse – he would have been in trouble with the Government.

I figured I was really making some progress, I mean getting a handle on this angel thing, when I realized that I had at least two serious problems. The first was, if angels use two of their wings to cover their faces, how do they see where they're going? And second, when angels "sit down," what in the world do they do with their wings? And you know something else that I learned from this angel? – we always think of angels as being "soft fuzzies," who bring messages of comfort and hope – like in this passage from Luke 2:9, where the angel of the Lord appeared to the shepherds and says, "Do not be afraid. I bring you good news of great joy that will be for all the people. Today in the town of David a Savior has been born to you; he is Christ the Lord."

Well, this angel at the tomb of Jesus didn't tell these Roman soldiers not to be afraid of him, in fact, he said, "Be afraid!" – "Be very afraid!" He scared the pants off these guys. (You know, I just remembered that Roman soldiers didn't wear pants, they wore those silly looking, pleated, leather things that just came down to their knees – but saying that the angel scared the "skirts" off of them seems a little inappropriate.)

So, I had learned at least two things about angels. First, all angels do not look alike, and second, they don't all act in the same way. Three more passages I want you to look at – no – I want you to *marvel* at.

Peter and the Angel
First, Acts 12:7

Suddenly an *angel of the Lord* appeared and a light shone in the cell. He struck Peter on the side and woke him up. "Quick, get up!" He said, and the chains fell off Peter's wrists. Then *the angel* said to him, "Put on your clothes and sandals." And Peter did so. "Wrap your cloak around you and follow me," *the angel* told him. Peter followed him out of the prison, but he had no idea that what *the angel* was doing was really happening; he thought he was seeing a vision. They passed the first and second guards and came to the iron gate leading to the city. It opened for them by itself, and they went through it. When they had walked the length of one street, suddenly *the angel* left him.

See what I mean about angels being "real"? This one pokes Peter in the side to wake him up, and then gives him all these instructions – and Peter isn't frightened at all – he doesn't even ask, "Who are you," because he doesn't believe it's really happening – he thinks it's a dream. I like that because it gives me hope for myself – because that is what I would think if an angel appeared to me – "this really isn't happening." And then, just about the time Peter began to realize that this was real – the angel leaves – which is just like an angel. I think I know what went through Peter's mind when he realized he wasn't dreaming – because that is what goes through everybody's mind when an event like this happens to him or her – he thought, "Here this incredible thing has happened to me and I can't tell anybody, because if I do they not only won't believe me – they'll think I'm crazy."

And then I came across three passages that are not only inform-ative – because they tell us things about angels in general – they are heartwarming and reassuring.

> "The angel of the LORD encamps around those who
> fear him, and he delivers them" PSALM 34:7.

> "See that you do not look down on one of these little ones.
> For I tell you that their angels in heaven always see the
> face of my Father in heaven" MATTHEW 18:10.

Jesus says that children have a "personal angel" who looks after their welfare, and although that's wonderful – it sort of made me sad because I'm not a child anymore and I wondered when "my angel" had left me?

But the most sweeping and reassuring passage I found was this one from Hebrews 1:14:

> "Are not all angels ministering spirits
> sent to serve those who will inherit salvation?"

The Hebrews author says that *all angels* serve the same function – they are "ministering spirits," and they "minister" to a very specific and exclusive group – "those who will inherit salvation." Now if you're a Christian, that just has to thrill you – and it did thrill me because I know that I have *my angel* back.

And here is one more, just in case you need something extra to warm your heart and lift your spirits. When you read it, if you're a Bible reader at all you'll say – "O, I've read that passage a lot of times" – and I'm sure you have – but have you "thought" about it? Have you tried to "imagine it"? If watching too much television hasn't totally robbed you of one of God's greatest gifts – the ability to "see in the mind" – use it as you read this passage from Luke 16:19-22.

Rich Man and Lazarus

> "There was a rich man who was dressed in purple and fine linen and lived in luxury every day. At his gate was laid a beggar named Lazarus, covered with sores and longing to eat what fell from the rich man's table. Even the dogs came and licked his sores. The time came when the beggar died – *and the angels carried him to Abraham's side.*
>
> The rich man also died and was buried."

"The angels came and carried Lazarus to Abraham's side." Isn't that a beautiful, heart warming thought? Doesn't that just almost make you want to die so you can be – "carried by angels to Abraham's side"?

Can you imagine lying on your hospital bed, wracked with pain from cancer eating away at your vital organs – drifting in and out of consciousness because of the drugs in your system – ten tubes running in and out of your body – people in white and green gowns coming into your room to check the monitors surrounding your bed – your loved ones grieving at your bedside – and then gradually you begin to realize that you don't hurt anymore – and you have a growing feeling of "wellness" and of – "motion."

You're afraid to open your eyes, so you start feeling around with your hands and you realize that your hospital bed isn't underneath you anymore – in fact there isn't *anything* underneath you anymore – but you feel these "hands" supporting you, and there is a soft, soothing, and sweet smelling breeze blowing. You finally summon up the courage to open your eyes and you see "faces," but these faces are not like any faces you've ever seen before. These are the strongest, healthiest, brightest, freshest, friendliest, most joyful and intelligent faces you've ever seen, and you say,

"Who are you?" And they say,

"We are the angels of God, and Ariel here is the one who has been assigned to you from the day you were born."

And you say, "Oh, what a blessing to meet you after all these years – I hope I haven't been too much trouble – thank you, thank you so very much, but where are you taking me?" And they say,

"To Abraham's side!"

And the realization that these are angels – real angels – and that this is really happening causes it to dawn on you that it's all true. It's All True! Everything you placed your faith in and built your life on is all true! Jesus is Lord, and there never has been, and there never will be any emotion – any feeling – any experience or realization that can compare to the everlasting joy of that one.

And you know, it isn't that I hadn't read or heard those passages before – the truth is I just – "blocked them out" – sort of pretended they weren't there – the way we all do with passages that make us uncomfortable – because they complicate our lives by destroying all of the nice, neat, perfectly square, "boxes" that we have our theology in.

Anyway, all this reading and thinking about angels caused me to look at myself and wonder why, after forty five years of preaching, I had never preached a sermon, taught a class, or written about angels? I thought, "If I'm supposed to be a 'Bible preacher,' and speak where the Bible speaks – why don't I preach about angels?" I hate questions like that. And I hate the answers even more, because the truth is that first, it's because I'm a little afraid of the "emotional distortions" that surround this topic, and second, because I'm afraid of what I don't "understand." And I think that what came crystal clear to me at this point was the most important lesson of all that I learned about angels. You see, we're not supposed to "understand" angels – any more than we're supposed to "understand" God – we're supposed to "believe" in them – and "wonder" about them – and try to imagine their glory.

And you know what else, reading those passages and thinking about angels, reminded me of some incidents from my childhood – and my life that I had never written down. And since that's what I do – write down stories from my life – and the lives of others – I wondered why I had never written down some of the most graphic memories I have? I think it's because I have been afraid of what they seem to imply and being misunderstood. But I believe the potential blessings outweigh the potential distortions, and so I wrote them down, along with some others and I want to share them with you.

May God bless you as you read,
and may He use these words
to cause you to stand in awe –
to marvel and wonder, and
to accomplish His purposes in your life.

I started praying again, a prayer born
of helplessness, desperation, and hope.
I said, "O dear God, please, please let someone
come – please send someone to help me.
Doug's hurt real bad and James went for help,
and he's been gone for hours and I'm all alone,
and I'm scared, and I don't know what to do"
– over and over I prayed the same prayer,
and I don't know how long it was,
but it seemed almost immediately,
I heard a voice say, "What's the trouble son?"

Oak Trees and Angels

The oak tree is gone now. I know exactly where it was – a person just doesn't forget a thing like that – and I have been back – and I have looked – and it is certainly gone. It was inevitable I know. It had grown too closely to the creek bank, and after two hundred and fifty years of spring floods that had ripped, and torn, and eroded the bank, exposing the tree's massive and twisted roots, causing it to lean precariously in spite of its great size – yes, I knew it was inevitable that some day it must fall. And yet, somehow I had hoped it would be there when I went back. After all, it had been there before the Revolutionary War, and it had been there through my childhood, and I wanted badly for it to be there now – but it was gone –

and not a trace of it remained.

The tree was important to me because it was the key to two, life – changing, but somewhat surrealistic childhood memories. My problem was that they happened so long ago, and memory is such a fickle thing, that I thought perhaps over the long years since they occurred, I might have exaggerated or distorted them. Or worse yet, I might even be mistaken about them ever happening – and somehow I thought that if the tree was still there – I might have more "confidence" in them, because they would be made more "real" by its presence.

And so I stood beside Rochester Road, looking at the spot where the tree had been, and tears filled my eyes, and I closed them, and I was a boy again, and it was summer – glorious, carefree, adventuresome, warm day, cool night, Michigan summer – and James and Doug and I were fishing at the creek.

Actually, James and Doug were not fishing, I was. They had no interest in fishing, they hadn't even brought fishing poles. When we separated, they said that they were going to wade downstream in the shallow water close to the shore and reach up into the holes under the overhanging bank to try to catch frogs, turtles, crayfish or bullheads. I slowly worked my way upstream, wading waist deep, searching tentatively for a foothold on the slippery, moss covered rocks, the lazy current tugging at my jeans, threatening to upset my precarious balance. I was trying to get in position to throw my worm into the deep hole under the bridge over Rochester Road, but my ten – foot cane pole, with the short piece of black fishing line tied to the end, forced me to get close. I finally made it, and I was catching some blue gills, rock bass, and an occasional bullhead, throwing them up on the bank to take home, when I heard James call me – "Hey John, come here, we figured out a way to climb the tree."

He didn't have to say which tree – there was only one tree anywhere in that area that we had not conquered – the oak tree. The reason we hadn't climbed it before was that the lowest branch was far out of our reach, and the girth of the tree was so great that our arms could not grasp it to "shinny" ourselves up to the first branch. The thought of actually conquering the oak tree was so tempting that I immediately began working my way back to the bank.

When I got to the tree, I discovered that Doug had tied a huge knot in one end of the long, heavy piece of rope he had found lying beside Rochester Road on the way to the creek. Somehow, he had succeeded in throwing the rope and wedging that knot in a fork of the lowest limb. By the time I got there, he was thirty feet up the tree and James was just going hand over hand up the rope, feet braced against the trunk, until he could grab the lowest limb.

By the time James was up the tree, Doug must have been sixty feet up and still climbing. I grabbed the rope and started up, but I was only about halfway to the first limb when I heard the branch that Doug was standing on crack and break. I heard his terror-stricken scream, and looked up just in time to see him fall – arms flailing, body twisting, hands grasping desperately. I watched in horror as he hit several small limbs, barely interrupting his rapidly accelerating descent – and then he fell sideways, with a dull, sickening thud, across a huge limb. The next sound he made was like a wheezing sigh, as all the air was forced suddenly from his lungs. And then his body crumpled and went all limp, and when he continued to fall, he fell loosely, his body flopping like a rag doll –

and he made no further sound.

It all happened so suddenly, I had no time to react, and his falling body missed me only by inches. He landed flat on his back, like a sack of concrete, and his body made a sound like you might hear when you drop an overripe watermelon. I jumped off the rope and was at his side in seconds. He lay just as he had fallen, face up – eyes wide open – but even a child could tell that he wasn't seeing anything. "Doug," I called his name in a terrified whisper – "Doug, are you all right?" There was no response – not even the flicker of an eyelid, or a motion of his hand.

I was soon joined by James who had scrambled recklessly down, and we stood in solemn silence, looking for a sign of life and wondering what we should do. James finally suggested that we get some water from the creek and throw it on his face to revive him. I thought that was a good idea and so I went and got my worm can, dumped out the worms, and filled it with water. We poured it in a steady stream over his face, and we talked to him and shook him gently –

there was no response at all.

We began to debate what we should do. James said that we ought to go for help, but we were at least two miles from home, maybe three. "He's dead," I said, "there's nothing we can do, but we can't just leave him, so we ought to try to get him home." James agreed, and so I grabbed one arm and James, the other, and we began dragging him back to Rochester Road in the hope that we could flag down a passing motorist.

Doug was much heavier than either of us, and I have no idea how long it took – but I'm sure it was at least ten minutes before we tugged, heaved, and pulled him up the steep bank to the road. We were sweating and exhausted, so we sat down beside the road to catch our breath. During this entire ordeal, Doug made no sound, his eyes remained wide open, but there was no life in them, and no motion of either hand or foot.

When we got our strength back, we decided to place Doug's body right next to the road while we tried to flag down passing motorists by yelling, waving, and pointing to the body. I guess they thought we were trying to play a prank on them, and they smiled and waved and drove on. There wasn't much traffic, so finally we dragged him across Rochester Road – his heels dragging and his head bumping cruelly on the pavement – with the idea of dragging him all the way to Spike Brown's house, which was the closest house where we knew anybody. The task was too much for us. We finally left him in the ditch beside the dirt road that led to Spike's house while we ran to see if someone was there, but there was nobody home.

We went back to Doug and talked more about what to do. We finally decided that I would stay with Doug and James would go for help. He took off running like a scared rabbit, but he was gone a long time. I sat in the ditch close to Doug, and I was just a boy, and I was scared, and I thought I ought to do something, so I held his limp hand and talked to him. Because I was a child of the church – raised in a deeply religious home – I decided that I would pray, because that is what my family always did when we were in trouble. So I knelt down right beside him – like my father did beside my bed at night – and I held both of his hands in mine, I closed my eyes tightly, and I prayed as fervent and heart-felt a prayer as I ever prayed in my life.

As I was praying, I felt a slight movement in Doug's fingers, and when I opened my eyes I happened to be looking right at his stomach and I saw it heave – and I knew he was alive. I looked immediately at his face, and there was light in his eyes – he recognized me! He even tried to say something – I saw his lips move, but no sound came out – and then his eyes closed for the first time –

and they never opened again.

I started praying again, a prayer born of helplessness, desperation, and hope. I said, "O dear God, please, please let someone come – please send someone to help me. Doug's hurt real bad and James went for help, and he's been gone for hours and I'm all alone, and I'm scared, and I don't know what to do" – over and over I prayed the same prayer, and I don't know how long it was, but it seemed almost immediately, I heard a voice say, "What's the trouble son?"

When I looked up – you must remember that I was kneeling in a ditch, at least two feet below the level of the road where the voice had come from – and when I looked up the first thing I saw was a big pair of tan work boots, they were worn, unlaced. As I raised my eyes, I noticed that whoever was wearing the boots had jeans on, and they were dirty, and they had holes in the knees. Continuing to look up, I saw what had been a white "T" shirt – and above the "T" shirt was the square jawed, sweating, muscular, smiling face of a huge black man. How can I tell you how big he appeared to me – he looked like Goliath. The "T" shirt could not hide the massive chest – his neck was as thick as a tree trunk and the short sleeves revealed bulging muscles.

He was unshaven, and rough looking, and although I had never been that close to a black man before, I had absolutely no fear of him whatsoever, because his smile was genuine and his voice was gentle and reassuring. But beyond that, the most important thing was that I believed with all my heart that he was God's answer to my prayer – he was an angel sent by God to help me.

He was a cement truck driver, and he had seen me holding Doug's hands and praying from Rochester Road, and he had guessed that something was wrong. I must have heard him stop the truck, because it was only a couple hundred feet from where I was, but I had been so intent on my prayer that I had paid no attention.

"What's wrong with your friend?" he asked again.

"He fell out of a tree," I blurted out, "and we thought he was dead, and we dragged him over here, but we couldn't go any further, and Spike's not home, so James went for help, and he's been gone for hours, and I've been praying – and he's not dead – see – he's breathing, and a minute ago he moved his fingers and he recognized me, and he tried to say something, but he couldn't, and he's hurt real bad, and I don't know what to do, and I've just been kneeling here beside him for a long time, holding his hand and praying, and then you showed up. Please help me!"

He asked where we lived and I told him, and he said he would go and get help because there was no place to put Doug in his truck, but just as he started back to his truck, Miss Watson's old black Dodge came around the corner real fast, and Doug's mother, and James and his mother, and my mother were in it. They all jumped out and started asking a whole bunch of questions at the same time, and I was trying to answer all of them at the same time, and Doug's mom knelt down in the ditch beside him, and she was holding his head in her arms, calling his name, and crying real hard. She kept saying, "Oh he's dead, he's dead, my Doug is dead," and I was trying to tell her that he wasn't – and the cement truck man said that what we needed to do was to get Doug to a doctor as fast as we could, and that made sense to everybody, so he just knelt down in the ditch and cradled Doug in his arms like he was a little baby, and carried him to Miss Watson's car and laid him very gently in the back seat, and Doug's mother got in the front seat and Miss Watson drove away with them to the hospital.

My mom, and James' mom, and James and I stood silently and watched Miss Watson's car drive out of sight. When we looked for the cement truck driver we discovered that he had already left without saying a word. We watched him drive away in a cloud of black diesel smoke. My mother asked me who he was, and I told her he was an angel sent by God to help me, and at first she looked at me with a funny expression on her face – like a frown – and she started to say something, but she stopped and thought for a minute, and then she said that she guessed maybe he was. And then James' mom said nobody had even thanked him, or asked him what his name was. And it occurred to me that I would never see him again.

The next day Doug's mom called and told my mom that Doug hadn't regained consciousness yet because he had a terrible concussion. She said that his back was broken in four places, and he was going to be in the hospital for a long time. That night, and for many nights after, my dad prayed for Doug before we ate and when he came to my room to say goodnight.

The next Saturday, my dad said that Doug's dad wanted me to take him to where it happened – but I told my dad that I didn't want to go to that place – not at all. But my dad said he was going, and James and his dad too, and it would be all right.

We showed them the tree, and the rope that was still hanging from it. They could see the broken limb where Doug fell, and Doug's dad said it must be at least seventy-five feet up. We showed them the trail in the leaves where we had dragged Doug, and Doug's dad got upset and said some mean things to James and me about how stupid that was – but my dad stood up for me and told him to be quiet – he said that he knew that he was upset, but he simply wouldn't allow him to talk to me like that. He said that we were just children and we couldn't possibly know any better. But it made me feel terrible because Doug's dad said that Doug wouldn't be so bad if we hadn't dragged him. My dad told him he didn't know anything about that, and that he ought to get on his knees and thank God that his son was alive, and that we had been with him, because if Doug had been alone he might have died.

I got my fishing pole, and then we took them across Rochester Road to the place where we had left Doug in the ditch while we ran to Spike Brown's house. I told them about how I had held his hands and prayed, and how he had moved his fingers and recognized me and tried to speak. I told them that while I was praying God had sent the cement truck driver, and I believed he was an angel – and Doug's dad laughed at me and he said there was no such thing as a black angel – which made my dad sort of mad – and he said that for all he knew all of God's angels were black, and he didn't care what color they were as long as God sent them. And he told me that he was proud of me, and that I had done just exactly right, and maybe it was my prayer that had saved Doug. Then Doug's dad broke down and cried, and he asked me to forgive him for saying mean things – he said that he was just upset about his son being hurt so badly, and he thanked me for being such a good friend and for praying for his son.

That night, when I said my prayers – I thanked God for giving me a father who would stick up for me – and I prayed for Doug – I prayed that he would be all right – and I hoped God would forgive me for being dumb and dragging Doug, and I hoped he wouldn't hold my stupidity against Doug and make him suffer for it. I told God that "just between us" the thing I was most grateful for was for answering my prayer and sending an angel to help me – and believing that changed my life –

and I hope it will change yours.

How can we pray "in faith" about matters
that we can see no way for God to respond to?
It seems to me that if we had a greater faith
in angels as, "ministering spirits sent to serve
those who will inherit salvation," we might
be more able to pray "in faith."

2
Ministering Spirits

"Are not all angels ministering spirits sent to serve
those who will inherit salvation?" HEBREWS 1:14

The Hebrews twelve passage that I referred to earlier says to us,
"But you have come to Mount Zion, to the heavenly Jerusalem, the
city of the living God.

You have come to thousands upon
thousands of angels in joyful assembly."

And I suppose that in order for that passage to have any meaning
at all we are going to have to believe in angels. At the church where I
preach, we sing a song called, "Holy Ground," and the words to one
of the verses are, "We are standing, on Holy Ground, and *I know that
there are angels all around."* Sometimes I wonder if we really believe
that there are "angels all around"?

I never see anybody looking for them!

After I began my study, I developed a sermon on angels, and in
that sermon I always tell either the story you just read, or the one that
follows. I have preached that sermon about twelve times in six different states now, and do you know what I have discovered? – no – of
course you don't – so I'm going to tell you. Almost everybody has an
"Angel Story." Folks come up to me after the sermon, and they wait
until there is no one around, and then they sort of pull me over to one
side, and they whisper – "Brother Smith, I want to tell you about
something that happencd to me, but you have to promise not to tell
anybody – I wouldn't want anybody to know."

And when they finish their story they always ask, "Do you believe that was an angel?" – as though they needed my confirmation. And I tell them that what "I" believe isn't important, what is important is what "they" believe, because what angels do is only important to those to whom they "minister." And I think that's the way it's supposed to be because I also notice that the people in the Bible who see angels don't run around screaming, "Hey everybody, I just saw an angel!"

Scripture says that angels are "ministering spirits," and it records the very practical roles they play in "ministering to" and "delivering" God's people. I wonder what "motivates" them. I mean do they just decide on their own initiative when to intervene – or do we have to "ask" for intervention – or does God foresee our difficulties and "instruct" them? Although all of these factors may be legitimate, I think that mainly they are God's way of responding to our prayers, because it seems to me that angels are often tied closely to answered prayer and to God's supernatural and providential intervention in our lives.

I do not at all mean that they need our instruction – I only mean that they need our "awareness" – our faith. I believe that their *ability* to intervene is severely restricted when folks don't "believe" or give credit to their intervention. It's sort of like the work of the Holy Spirit – His ability to lead, convict, intercede, inform, motivate, and guide us is severely restricted in those who refuse to acknowledge His real presence within them. It is not that He *cannot* do more – it is that He *will not* do more.

I am beginning to suspect that prayer is much more practical and powerful than I ever believed. Why would Jesus say, "Men ought always to pray and never give up"? I wonder why He gave us that instruction – especially that part about, "never giving up." I find that I give up all too easily – especially when it comes to prayer. If something doesn't happen pretty quickly, I either try to solve the problem myself, or else I go through some rationalization process that allows me to accept defeat.

Truthfully, I've always been a little *dissatisfied* with my prayer life

– it just never lived up to my expectations. For most of my life I found it easier to believe that God was going answer *certain types* of prayers more than others. What I mean is, if I prayed for rain – or even for someone who was sick – I didn't have much trouble believing that God at least "could" answer, because I *understood the process* by which He might do that. With rain, all He has to do is move a few clouds around. Sick people are easy – if they're not too sick – all He has to do is help the doctors prescribe the right medicine, or cut in the right place.

But if I prayed for patience, or to be more kind, faithful, or to get rid of certain sins in my life, or be more holy – doubt crept in because I had no understanding of "the process" by which God might do that – I mean – how is God going to make me more holy? I knew He wasn't going to perform brain surgery and turn a screw in my head, and although I continued to pray for those things, because I was "supposed to," I did not pray "in faith" – I only gave "lip service" to those prayers. I think that in my case, my "dissatisfaction" with my prayer life was caused by my concept of God. My view of the "cause and effect" aspect of the circumstances of both my physical and spiritual life was so rational and "evolutionary" that I had little faith in God's ability to work physically in this world.

What I mean by "lip service" can be demonstrated by some of the prayer songs we sing. When we sing –

> "Father hear the prayer we offer,
> nor for ease that prayer shall be,
> but for strength that we may ever
> live our lives courageously."

We need to ask ourselves, do we really believe that God is going to "do something" that will lead us to live courageous lives? And if so

– do we believe that He has any practical way of doing it? My point is that if we have no faith in God's ability to work in this world – to circumvent "natural causes" – we find it almost impossible to believe that He can answer us, which takes the "heart" out of our prayers, leaving them empty.

When we sing,

> "Jesus, let us come to know you –
> let us see you face to face."

How is Jesus going to *answer* that prayer? What is Jesus going to "do" that will allow us to "know Him" and see Him "face to face"? Do we believe that it is *possible* to see Jesus, "face to face"? If it isn't possible – if we don't *believe* – why pray for it? If it is possible – how is it possible? When the Jews are stoning Stephen to death in Acts seven – just before he dies he yells – "look, I see the heavens opened and Jesus standing at God's right hand!" But when the Jews looked they didn't see anything. Do you think he was hallucinating? Do we *believe* that the heavens were really open, and Jesus was really standing at God's right hand? If what Stephen saw was really there, why couldn't those Jews who were trying to kill him see it? That is an important question and we need to be very careful how we answer. Could the answer have something to do with the difference between Stephen's *faith* and his murderers' faith? Could the answer have something to do with the fact that Stephen had just said that they were, "uncircumcised in heart and ears, and do always resist the Holy Spirit?"

When we ask God to give us a safe journey, or to protect our children, or to help us be more loving, kind, patient, or faithful – do we *believe* that God has a way of answering those prayers?

James tells us that if our prayers are going to be answered, we must pray "in faith" or "believing," and he says that if we "doubt" we have no reason to believe that God is going to respond. The question is, "How can we do that?" How can we pray "in faith" about matters that we can see no way for God to respond to? It seems to me that if we had a greater faith in angels as, "ministering spirits sent to serve those who will inherit salvation," we might be more able to pray "in faith."

Take the story I just told you as an illustration. There I was, an eight-year-old boy, totally helpless, scared and alone, kneeling in a ditch beside my hurt friend, asking God to help me. How is God going to respond to my prayer? At the time, I didn't think about *how* He might do it – and I didn't care either – I prayed in desperate, child-like *faith*. But as an adult, I can't help thinking about "how" God is going to respond. Here's what I think happens. I think that when I prayed, God looked around at the angels who, as we read earlier are, "always before his face" – and He pointed at one of them and said,

"Ariel!"

"Yes sir," the angel responded.

"Ariel, come here, I have a job for you."

"Great, what do You want me to do?"

"Listen, there's an eight-year-old boy praying for help for his friend who just fell out of a tree and broke his back. He's kneeling in a ditch, desperate, scared, and he's alone – I want you to go and help him."

"Where is he?"

"He's right there – that's Rochester Road I'm showing you – it's in Michigan."

"What do You want me to do, Lord – if I just show up he'll die of fright," Ariel says.

"Tell you what, grab a cement truck and just drive past, pretend that you just happened to see him.

"Where am I going to get a cement truck?"

"You of all beings should know that if I can make a universe, a cement truck isn't much of a challenge."

"I'm sorry, I don't know when I'm going to learn that You can do things like that, but You may have forgotten that I don't know how to drive."

"I don't 'forget' anything, but don't worry about that, most humans don't know how to drive either – that's why they kill each other every day on their roads – you'll fit right in. Now remember, the mission is not the boy who's hurt – all I want you to do is help get him to the hospital, he'll be fine – it's the boy whose praying that I'm concerned about. This is the first time that he's really turned to Me for help – he needs an angel right now, and he's still so young he'll believe in you. He doesn't know this yet, but about fifty years from now he's going to remember this event and start telling people about it."

Every Sunday, at the church where I preach, we ask people to turn in prayer requests, and at the end of the service we read them and pray. I don't recall a single Sunday when at least one person hasn't turned in a request for safe travel for himself or a loved one. Praying for safe travel is very popular because everybody thinks they're going to arrive safely anyway – I mean if they didn't – they wouldn't go. Besides, there is no loss of face involved with prayers like that, like there is with confessing a need for help to overcome sin in our lives.

One thing I have learned about praying for safe travel is that we only pray for people who are going over a *hundred miles*. No, really, nobody ever asks us to pray for them as they drive to the grocery store or the football game. It's because we think that we can handle anything under a hundred miles by ourselves.

I fear that often we pray those prayers rather mechanically, because I notice that when they arrive safely we seldom fall to our knees in gratitude and praise God for the "providential intervention" that got us there. Instead we talk about what "good drivers" we are, and how we never even "saw an accident," or had a "close call." My goodness – what kind of faith is that? Does God have to allow us to have a "brush with death" to make us realize that we may have had a thousand "close calls," we simply never saw or believed that God's angels were answering our prayers – moving about three miles ahead of us – "clearing the way."

I realize fully that this is a "dangerous" area –
subject to much abuse,
but abuse does not justify unbelief.

I believe that the more we study our Bibles – the more we dedicate ourselves to godly living and godly thinking – the more we come to "know Him" and live in conformity to His will – the more "effective" our prayers will be because we will be more able to ask "in faith" – and the more "angels" we will see.

He could not climb out, especially in
his exhausted, weakened condition,
and the water was over his head.
There were no tree roots, no vines,
nothing to grip, and his enemy now
was the cold and the creeping numbness
that was driving the feeling from his extremities.
He tried desperately to dig his fingers into
the dirt of the creek bank, but it was useless.
He realized that he was helpless –
that he wasn't going to make it, and
in desperation he cried out loud –
"O God, Help Me!"

3
You're an Angel to Me

I feel duty bound to tell my readers that I have written this next story deliberately in the "third person." I did that hoping to prevent you from asking me if this "really happened." Although this story is "rooted" in fact – it is much more "creative" than most of my stories. I wonder if anybody ever came up to Jesus and asked Him, "Was there really a prodigal son who did all of those things, and did his father really take him back?" I think Jesus would have said, "You have asked the wrong question, and you have missed the whole point. Whether or not there was a prodigal son doesn't matter – what matters is if you know more truth about God now." He didn't tell the story to "entertain" – He told it to "reveal truth" by placing it in a real human setting.

I said earlier that the oak tree "held *two* lasting, life-changing memories" for me. This is the other. It took place on a Saturday, about nine months later, in late March, 1946. Doug had come home from the hospital in a full-body cast made of plaster. It went from his hips to right under his armpits. It was about an inch thick, and it must have been very heavy. He wore it for the rest of the summer. After a few days, he tried to play with us, but his movements were extremely awkward and he tired easily. The thing I remember vividly was that where his armpits rubbed against the cast – they looked like raw meat. The plaster cast was eventually replaced with a leather apparatus that had belts and straps and buckles, which he wore for several weeks. Doug and his family moved, sometime during the school year – and I never saw him again.

As you can well imagine, over the months, the memory of Doug's fall and our fear of the oak tree faded completely away, and my friends and I replaced Doug's rope with some boards that we nailed to the tree to make it easier to climb.

I know this event happened on a Saturday, because if it hadn't been Saturday, I would have been on my way to school on this bright morning. Because it was Saturday, I was laying on top of that huge lowest limb, that I have referred to, which extended horizontally out over the water of the creek.

It was the time of the spring thaw. On every hillside that faced South, the direct beams of the spring sun had begun to penetrate the snow with increasing intensity, transmitting their warmth to last year's dark, rotting vegetation which lay beneath. The vegetation absorbed that warmth, instead of reflecting it as the snow did, and transmitted it upward, and the snow nearest to the ground began to melt. Tiny drops of water, collected under the snow in little rivulets, some no more than a quarter of an inch wide, but they trickled to other small rivulets, which in turn collected and crept along unseen under the snow, and those collected rivulets became small streams. The moving water slowed and froze at night, but each day it thawed, and every part of that moving water system grew larger and more forceful as it pushed its way to its objective. Normally, the tiny streams began to reach the creek in mid- to late March.

The creek was a rather insignificant tributary of the Clinton River, which flowed to the Great Lake Huron, named after a legendary tribe of Indians who had once roamed the area. The creek, completely frozen, except in some of its deepest holes, began to respond to the surge of the incoming water with a change of its own. When the ice had first formed on the creek, back in November, the water was immediately below the surface of the ice. All winter long the water level had dropped, until it lay several inches below the ice. As the new, warmer water began to find its way into the creek, that air space immediately below the ice was filled, and the ice cap actually began to "lift and float" as the water began to push its way out under the edges of the ice near the banks. With each afternoon thaw and each nightly freeze, the ice cap surged, heaved, cracked and finally broke and the creek began to flow. Once it began to flow, the moving water kept the middle of the creek open, and the only ice to be found was near the edges.

Now changes began to take place more rapidly. Each day, the melting snow brought greater quantities of warm water, rushing with ever greater insistence and determination to the creek. The small creek rushed to the river, and the river, along with countless others, rushed to the Great Lake Huron, and the rushing rivers carried the fragments of last year's vegetation, and the thawing bodies of worms, frogs and crayfish that had buried themselves in the mud of the creek banks to survive the long winter. This sent a message to all the things that lived in the lake that spring had come.

The fish awakened from the torpid sleep of the winter months, and they moved to the mouths of the rivers to feed and then begin their ancient reproductive journey. Only God knows why the fish couldn't just spawn in the lake, but they couldn't, and that is why the boy was there. He was there to do what his ancestral generations of fishermen had been doing for thousands of years – he was there to spear the spawning fish.

On this Saturday, snow still covered both banks of the creek, and ice still formed at the edges. The water was crystal clear and bitterly cold. It was the time for the first run of spring suckers from Lake Huron. The limb the boy was on, jutted out right over the shallow, swiftly moving water between two rather deep pools. He leaned out to his right, over the water, his body delicately balanced by his left leg, which was dangling from the other side of the limb, and his left arm, which was wrapped around a small limb which projected from the limb he was lying on. As the suckers moved upstream from one pool to the next, they had to pass through the shallow, swiftly moving water of the riffle beneath him.

He twisted his body, squirming and crawling clumsily even further out on the limb, increasing his already precarious position. His movements were made even more awkward because he was holding a long, wooden pole in his right hand. Actually, it wasn't a "pole," it was a "handle," and it was much longer than he was tall. Attached to one end of the handle was an old, heavy, five-pointed, cast-iron spearhead – and although the head was pitted from rust, the points were shiny, recently filed to razor edges. At the other end, a hole had been drilled through the handle, and a rope had been threaded through it. The rope was wound around his wrist so that if he dropped the spear, he could retrieve it.

It was about midmorning. The boy had been there since daylight, and four shiny, snow crusted suckers lay gasping and bleeding on the bank. He only had thin, brown Jersey gloves on, and he didn't have the kind of thermal clothing that is necessary to keep body heat in when there is no activity. He was numb with cold, especially his hands and feet. When he had speared the suckers, he had to remove them from the spear, and of course he had gotten his hands wet and bloody – now he could barely feel them. He decided to climb down and warm himself.

Just as he made the first move, he saw a large, dark shadow move from the depths of the lower pool. He held his breath and remained motionless, peering intently at the spot where he thought he had seen the movement. Perhaps he was mistaken, it might have simply been a chunk of ice, or more likely, a last year's sodden oak leaf finally dislodged and moving sluggishly with the current along the bottom. And then he saw it again –

it was a fish!

He knew it wasn't a sucker. He had seen some large ones, even one that weighed six pounds, but this fish was much larger, and differently formed. When it moved closer to the shallow water of the riffle, he recognized the long, powerful, torpedo-shaped body as that of a northern pike – a huge one. It was before the time when they usually came. Normally they stayed in the deeper water of the river until after the first spring rain, which swelled the creek and made the water so murky that they easily eluded him. He had seen many of them, but never in this creek, and never that size.

As the big fish moved easily into the shallows just below the riffle between the two pools, he was astonished at its size. He had seen the head of a twelve-pound pike that Albert had caught in Wing Lake, in fact, the head was still nailed to the door of Albert's well house, but this fish was much larger than that, more than twice as big – in fact – it was the biggest fish he had ever seen.

He tingled with excitement, and momentarily forgot the creeping numbness in his hands and feet, but only momentarily. The fish, having tested the depth of the riffle, turned sideways slowly and allowed the current to carry it back to the lower pool, where it gradually submerged. The moment's exhilaration over, the boy began to feel more acutely the tingling numbness in his limbs.

He realized that he could not stay where he was much longer. He also knew that if he moved, he would probably lose all chance of spearing the fish. He was astute enough to realize that even if he stayed and succeeded in spearing the fish, he would likely lose his precarious balance and fall into the creek. The fall didn't worry him – it was less than six feet – and the creek wasn't deep where he was, less than eighteen inches, so there was no great danger of drowning – but he knew that the icy water would soak his clothes and fill his boots. The thought of a two-mile walk home in freezing weather and trying to explain what happened to his mother made him decide that, if the fish did not come immediately, he would take his chances and climb down.

But the fish *did* come immediately.

The great pike, once it made up its mind to move to the next pool, came with a rush, and it passed directly beneath him. The fish was so large that its dorsal fin was out of the water. The boy knew exactly where to position the spear, and he plunged it with all of his strength just ahead of that fin, as close to the back of the head as possible. His goal was to kill the fish immediately, either by breaking the spine or puncturing the lung sack. He hit the fish in the right spot, but his position on the limb did not allow him to use his full weight, and the numbness in his hands and arms betrayed him. The center spear point hit the spine, but it lacked the necessary force to snap it. Instead, it glanced off, sinking deep and locking into the flesh. The points on either side drove themselves into the flesh on both sides of the spine. The fish was securely speared, and its life was over, but death would not come until it had exhausted its considerable strength.

In a desperate attempt to free itself of the spear, the fish exploded into a frenzy of action, hurtling itself totally out of the water, its tail slapping the surface, churning it to foam – nearly turning itself inside out. Its weight alone might have pulled the boy from his perch, but coupled with its crazed lunging, he simply had to either turn loose of the spear or fall to the creek. The rope, wrapped around his wrist, would not allow him to turn loose even if he wanted to, and besides, the spear was a prized possession, and while there was life in his body, he would not turn loose of it, and so he fell. He landed face down in the shallow, freezing water. The water partially absorbed the shock of the fall and shielded his body from the rocks of the riffle, but he was still stunned, and the freezing water immediately saturated his clothes and filled his boots. The fall also caused him to lose his grip on the spear, and the fish would have easily escaped except for the rope. The pressure of the constantly thrashing, driving fish prevented him from freeing his wrist of the rope, and his main thought was not to get free anyway, but to kill the fish and save his priceless spear.

He reached with his left hand and grasped the spear handle, drew it to him, and gripped it with both hands. He clung desperately to it, and tried to get to his feet. The frantic thrashing of the fish, his inability to use his legs and feet, the slippery rocks of the riffle, and his sagging, waterlogged clothes prevented him from doing so.

The instinctive drive of the fish was to get to the safety of the deep water of the upper pool. The boy did everything in his power to prevent it. Once, he succeeded in getting to his knees, but the fish jerked so hard that he lost his balance and fell forward on his stomach. What he didn't realize was that his stumbling attempts to get to his feet were actually propelling him forward, and helping the fish to reach its objective.

When he realized that his body was no longer bumping on the rocks, and his feet were unable to catch on anything, he knew that he was in the deep water of the upper pool – water which was over his head – and the swimming fish was now actually towing him forward. The leather boots on his feet were like lead weights. He was numb and exhausted, and he knew that he had done all he could – that he had to give up and try to get to the bank. The exhausted fish finally slowed its movements, and he was able to release the rope from his wrist. He knew the fish would die, and perhaps the handle of the spear would float well enough to allow him to find it.

The fish and the boy, locked together in this life and death struggle, gave up at about the same time. The crazed lunging of the mortally wounded fish had finally forced one of the spear points into the lung sack, and it died almost immediately. The boy was closer to the bank of the creek than to the shallow water of the riffle, so he began a slow motion, awkward, dog-paddling attempt to reach it. It wasn't far, ten – fifteen feet perhaps, and he reached it, but he was totally spent.

His problem now was that the creek made a turn here, and over the years the rushing water had undercut the bank, which was vertical. He could not climb out, especially in his exhausted, weakened condition, and the water was over his head. There were no tree roots, no vines, nothing to grip, and his enemy now was the cold and the creeping numbness that was driving the feeling from his extremities. He tried desperately to dig his fingers into the dirt of the creek bank, but it was useless. He realized that he was helpless – that he wasn't going to make it, and in desperation he cried out loud –

"O God, Help Me!"

The memory of the "angel" that God had sent a few months earlier, when he was in desperate trouble only a couple of hundred yards from this very place, flashed before his mind, and because he was a child – with a child's faith – he prayed "believing," and this story would end here – along with his life – if not for a most unusual set of circumstances.

Obviously all of this happened in much less time than it takes to tell, or read about it. It's amazing really, how little time and how small a space human drama fills – how thin the threads that hold life from death are. This whole epic struggle had filled a space of no more than three or four minutes in history, and occupied a geographical area of no more than fifteen square yards. You need to realize that, in order to appreciate the "improbability" of the next series of events – events that the boy had no more knowledge of than if they had happened in Arkansas.

Actually, it's the kind of thing that happens every day, but in less dramatic fashion. Almost everybody has either had it happen to them or heard about someone traveling two thousand miles to a town they have never been to before, and meeting their next-door neighbor, or someone equally familiar, on the street. It happens somewhere in the world every day, I suppose, but we are always astonished by it. How many conversations begin with the phrase, "You simply won't believe what happened!" Which of course means exactly the opposite, because the storyteller would be highly indignant if indeed when he finished, his listener said, "I don't believe a word of it."

A young man named Ed, who was a physical education instructor and junior high football coach in Rochester, Michigan, was traveling to Royal Oak on his day off. He was going to a gathering of area football coaches to set the playing schedule for the next year, and to learn about the changes made in summer practice restrictions. The tree, and the limb that the boy was on, was plainly visible from Rochester Road, and he had noticed him perched there on the previous Saturday, when he had been making the same trip. He had marveled, not only at the creative idea of spearing fish from the limb, but at the dedication it took to be where he was at a time when every other boy his age was at home in a warm bed.

On this day, he had left a little early, because he planned to stop and talk to the boy if he was there. There are two explanations for this. First, he was interested in young people, particularly in one who would be up at daylight on a freezing Saturday morning to spear a few suckers. Second, and by far the strongest of the two – this would only be understood by a dedicated fisherman – was that he was a fisherman, and so he shared that insatiable curiosity that is a part of every fisherman's mentality – the desire to know if another fisherman was having any luck.

As he approached the bridge that crossed the creek, he slowed, and seeing the boy laying on the limb he pulled his car off the road and parked in a small turnout. He got out, crossed the road, and started in his direction. Actually, he did not see him fall, because when he got out of the car, he was out of sight. Only after he had crossed the road and started down the creek bank, did he notice that the limb was empty. The tree was perhaps a hundred or so feet from the road, and he thought the boy might have climbed down.

As he made his way through the snow and around the brush that grew at the edge of the road and down the creek bank, he realized that the snow was much deeper, and the brush much thicker than he had anticipated – he wasn't dressed for it – and he was about to change his mind and go back when he heard the splashing and thrashing of the water and the boy's cry for help right below him.

He rushed to the high bank to see what had happened, and saw the boy, just as he was giving up his struggle. He grabbed a dead limb and extended it to him. "Grab the limb," he shouted. The boy tried, but he was too weak, his fingers were too numb to grasp it. "I want to," he said, "but I can't." Ed never hesitated, he jumped off the bank into the water – which only came to his chest – he grabbed the boy and began making his way downstream. When he reached shallower water, he picked him up, cradling him in his arms, made his way carefully to the bank, and began the walk back to the car. The boy was not unconscious – he was numb and exhausted – but he was not unconscious.

"My spear," he said, "you've got to help me get my spear."

"We can come back for it later, right now, I've got to get you warm," he said.

"Please," the boy said, "I'm very grateful, you are the answer to my prayer and you saved my life, but please put me down, I'm sure I can walk."

He put the boy down gingerly, sure that he would fall immediately, and he was amazed that not only did he stand up, he began to take a few shaky, stumbling steps back in the direction of the creek to get his spear.

It is amazing really, sometimes beyond belief, how the human will can not only overcome overwhelming physical circumstances, but also dominate the will of others – even those older and wiser. Ed found himself, against all reason, soaking wet and freezing, following a pint-sized boy, whom he had just saved from drowning, back to the creek to try and find his spear.

It was the handle they saw. The fish, its air sack punctured, had drowned, and the weight of the iron spear had caused it to sink. The opposite end of the spear handle was sticking up about two inches above the surface of the water. Ed tried to tangle the end of the limb he had extended to the boy in the rope attached to the handle, but failed.

"I can't reach it," he said, "we'll have to come back after it."

"You're already cold and wet," the boy reasoned, "you might as well get it now, it won't be any easier later when you're warm and dry."

As he waded back in to retrieve the spear, Ed must have asked himself why he was doing this. As a man, he wasn't too happy about it, he would have to go back home, change clothes, and explain to his wife – which is no easy thing – besides – he would miss most of the coaches' meeting. But as a *fisherman*, he would have gotten the spear even without the boy's insistence. Yes, he would have waded back into that freezing water to get it – *because he wanted to see the fish* – and equally importantly –

he wanted to tell the story.

He marveled at the fish's size. It was the largest pike he had ever heard of. They picked up the suckers and made their way as rapidly as possible to the warmth of the car. Ed carried the fish, and the boy carried the spear. They had a difficult time figuring out how to get the spear in the car, and they finally had to let the handle stick out one of the rear windows.

As they drove away the boy said,

"How did you happen to be there?" And after Ed explained he asked, very shyly – almost secretively,

"Are you an angel?" Ed looked at the boy, and seeing that he was serious said,

"No, I'm not an angel."

"If you are, you can tell me," he said, "and I promise I won't tell anyone, if that's important. The last time God sent an angel to help me, he left before I had a chance to tell him how grateful I was, and I didn't want that to happen again."

He looked at the boy and said, "What do you mean – the last time? How many times have you fallen out of that tree?" The boy explained about his friend who had fallen out of the tree and the cement truck driver who was an angel sent by God, and he told him about how he had prayed just before he showed up.

"That's quite a story, but no, son, I assure you that I am no angel.

When I was a little younger than you my mother used to call me, 'her little angel,' but no one has called me that in years – and probably for good reason."

"But you *could* be an angel," the boy insisted, maybe when God sends you down here to help us you forget you're an angel until you go back. Maybe you just don't remember right now."

"Son, God knows, I wish I was, but if I was an angel, my wife would be the most surprised and disappointed person on earth. I'm just a junior high teacher and football coach – and I'm not very good at that."

By this time they were at the boy's house, and as he got out of the car he said stubbornly, "Well, even if you're not an angel to you – you're an angel to me."

The God of Scripture has been manipulating
both circumstances and people to fulfill
His purposes from the beginning of time –
and He continues to do the same thing today.
We are all clay in the hands of the Master Potter.
Events like this do not prove that God only works
through "natural" forces and circumstances –
it only proves that there are "all kinds of angels."

All Kinds of Angels

I think we need to ask ourselves if the church assembles only to retell the "old stories": the flood, the fall of Jericho, and the crossing of the Jordan – do we assemble simply to celebrate the wonderful things that God *has done* in the lives of those who lived in the distant past – or does the church also assemble to tell the "new stories" of what God *is doing* in our lives in the present? Is God still performing His mighty works? Is He still delivering? Is He still sending His angels to heal – to protect – to empower and lead? Is He still conspicuously at work in our lives and in this world?

How we answer that question is extremely important, because it has a dramatic impact on *how* we pray – *how often* we pray – *what* we pray for – and most importantly if we pray *in faith*.

The explanation I gave in the last story of how Ed "happened" to come to this boy's assistance was in no way intended to discredit the "divine intervention" – the "angel" aspect of the story – or to reduce the "wonder" of it. Ed had no idea that he was an "angel" – and of course he wasn't in the sense of "Ariel" in the first story. He had no clue that God had been providentially "ordering his life" for months so that he would be in this place at this time to answer this boy's prayer. If he had appeared two minutes later it would have been too late – it wasn't a matter of luck, coincidence, or fate – it was *divine providence*. Many things might have happened to prevent him from being there at exactly thc right moment: a last-minute telephone call, a cancellation of the meeting, sickness, a flat tire, a missed traffic light – or a thousand others. But by the grace of God – nothing did – and Ed became one of God's "unwitting" angels.

The God of Scripture has been manipulating both circumstances and people to fulfill His purposes from the beginning of time – and He continues to do the same thing today. We are all clay in the hands of the Master Potter. Events like this do not prove that God only works through "natural" forces and circumstances – it only proves that there are

"all kinds of angels."

Sometimes the angels God sends are heavenly beings who appear in earthly form – like the one who came to shove the rock away from the tomb of Jesus – or like Ariel in the first story. In my experience those angels have been extremely rare – only "appearing" on random occasions; however the problem may simply be that we do not "see" them, because as adults we have become more "rational" and our scientifically trained faculties have blinded our eyes to spiritual truth. It may also be that although the role "real angels" play is very spectacular, it may not have as much long-term impact on our lives as the role played by other types of angels.

Sometimes, for reasons perceived only through His own wisdom, God sends "real people" – like Ed – who are no less angels – to play a single, momentary role in our lives and are never seen again – and I believe that by far these are the most common types of angels. They are simply people that we know, but we would never think of as "angels." It's easy to "pooh – pooh" things like this because they are so "common," and we like our "angels" to be more spectacular and effervescent, but I believe that God can use the most unlikely and even unwilling people to accomplish His purposes.

The Bible has many stories that demonstrate how God used people, like Pharaoh, without their knowledge to influence both history and the lives of people who were praying for help. There is a fascinating story in Judges chapter six where Moses says of the Israelites, because they "did evil" in God's eyes, that for seven years God "gave them into the hand of the Midianites." After seven years (do you wonder why it took them so long?) the Israelites "cried out to the Lord for help." God responds by sending them a "prophet" – a preacher. I'm sure they said, "Lord, we don't think you understand our situation – we don't need a preacher – *we need help*!"

But of course God does not answer our prayers by sending us what we "want – He answers us by sending us what we "need," and at this moment what Israel needed was a preacher, because the preacher is the one who explains the problem to them. "Your problem is not the Midianites" – God says, "I can deal with the Midianites before breakfast – your problem is that, "you have not listened to me." And just who is this "preacher?" We are never told his name – but we do know that he is "sent by God" – and that he "ministers" to God's people – and that means that he was an "angel" – whether in the sense of a "heavenly messenger" or an earthly one. I tend to think of that preacher as being a "heavenly messenger" because in that same chapter is the detailed account of the "angel" who comes to Gideon.

That example could be multiplied by a thousand. Not all of these are "angels" in the sense that we normally think of them – like Ariel – but the principle is exactly the same.

I believe there are also angels who enter our lives and stay for long periods of time, fulfilling God's purposes and answering our prayers over an extended period of time – even for years. One of those "angels" in my life was a preacher named L.C. Utley. Although I'm sure that he did not specifically intend to be, and unfortunately, it was many years after he died that I began to think of him in that way, he certainly was used by God to provide the answers to many of my prayers.

Wouldn't it be wonderful if we all thought of *ourselves* as God's angels – as part of His providential working on this earth? Wouldn't it make us change our attitudes toward those we meet? That is, if we thought that God had placed us in their company as "ministering servants?" Wouldn't it make us look for more opportunities to impact people's lives for the sake of the gospel?

He also taught me something intangible –
he taught me a side of God that I had not
learned elsewhere – the gentle, kind, loving
side of God. In some of the churches
I attended as a young man, I learned the
"facts" about God – and that is important –
but L.C. Utley helped me to experience God,
and he created a hunger in me for Godliness.
He made me long for God as the
deer pants for the water.

5
A Prayer for Holiness

Most of the time when we pray, we want immediate answers. And when those answers don't come within a short-time span – or in the way we want them to come – we say, "Oh well, I didn't think it would work anyway." And we either try to solve the problem by other means, or we give up and forget that we ever prayed.

Many prayers, by their very nature, demand a "long-term" response. For example – prayers for things like patience, to be more loving, to have a better heart, to deal with besetting sins – or for "holiness" in this case, cannot be answered in a single, spectacular incident, although we wish they could.

When I was a small boy, I became intrigued with the idea of "holiness." I believe it was the result of listening to my mother read stories to me about Samson and the Philistines, David and Goliath, Daniel in the lion's den, and Shadrach, Meshach, and Abednego in the fiery furnace. Those stories filled me with an intense desire to be noble, brave, and heroic – in the old and true sense of self-sacrifice, of laying my life on the line for the things that I believed in. I wanted to be *good* – in the sense of standing for the right against all odds – of being internally and completely good, of *not wanting* to do bad things.

Yes, I wanted very badly to *experience* holiness, and so I began praying to God to help me to be holy, but since I had no idea of how He might do that, I had no idea of what to look for in terms of an answer. In fact, I'm not sure I expected one. That prayer continued for many years. I do not mean that I prayed for it every day, no, at times I drifted far from it; and sometimes months would pass before something would happen to rekindle the old desire. What follows is a brief outline of that journey so you can better understand how God answered my prayer over a period of years through His angel – His "ministering servant," L.C. Utley.

I think that at the beginning, my ideas of what constituted holiness were very romantic – associated not only with the Biblical characters I mentioned earlier, but with books I had read about Robin Hood, or King Arthur and the knights of the roundtable – of Sir Lancelot searching for the Holy Grail – of slaying dragons, rescuing fair maidens (no one ever rescued an ugly one), and converting the infidels. As a boy I dreamed of going to foreign lands to find infidels to convert – and it was a great comfort to me when I grew up to realize that there were many of them in my hometown.

I honestly believe that I pursued holiness for its own sake, and out of a pure heart, until I reached junior high, but about the time that puberty set in, I began to see holiness as the "means to an end," rather than something to be pursued for its own glory. I am ashamed to say it now, but I am convinced that this happened because it was at this time in my life that I began to be

aware of myself.

That awareness did not at first completely deter me in the quest for holiness, it only made me alter my motivation. I no longer sought holiness because I hungered for righteousness – I sought it as the means to a selfish end. I was a "child of the church," I was born and raised as a child of the church. The church was my world and because I was a child of the church – and because I was now "aware of myself" – I began to see that holiness was the way to be "successful" – to be "recognized" in the church. I decided that if being holy was the way to get those things – then I would be holy. And so I began to do "holy things" – like leading singing and prayer, asking questions in class, memorizing Bible verses, and giving "talks." And the church rewarded me by showering attention on me.

But it was also about this time that I began to see that my "church world" was a very small world – and its ability to reward me was also small. I began to discover another world – a much larger one – a world with far greater ability to reward me. And so I began to pursue that world.

The first "thing" that captured my attention was sports: baseball, football and hockey, to be exact. I devoted myself to sports, my time and my energy. I sacrificed all other things in order to pursue sports, because I believed that success at sports would bring me the "feelings" of recognition, power, popularity, and even internal satisfaction that I so much desired. Sports took me further from my pursuit of holiness and the "Kingdom of God" than anything except the second "thing" – cars, *fast cars* to be exact.

I grew up in and around Detroit, Michigan, in the days of what were called the "muscle cars." I wanted to have the fastest car in town. I believed that if my car was the fastest – if I could beat everybody in a quarter-mile drag race – I would have the recognition, the power, the popularity that I so desperately wanted. Of all the things that interrupted my pursuit of holiness – cars were
the most useless of all.

The third "thing" was *girls*, not *fast* girls exactly, but *pretty* girls. When I "discovered" girls, they occupied my attention in a more complete and lasting way than either sports or cars. Yes – girls became the all-consuming "thing." I wanted to be recognized, popular, and successful with girls.

My early pursuit of holiness for its own sake did not leave me in one day – no – it's never that simple, and no matter how far I drifted from it, things would happen that called me back to that glorious aspiration I had once had. Sometimes it would be one of Brother Utley's sermons that "got through" – most often it would be one of the great hymns that we sang, hymns like – "Jesus Keep Me Near The Cross," or, "More Holiness Give Me." Sometimes I would see my mother praying with her Bible open on her lap – and I would feel so convicted of my hypocrisy that I would long for those days when my desires were more pure.

Sometimes, when I was under conviction, I would go to God in an absolute agony, desperate over my failures. I would plead with Him with tears to help me to have a better heart – to help me to be like my mother, or to be a "man after God's own heart" – like David – yes – that was it, I wanted to be like David and I often wondered, as long periods of time passed and no help seemed to come, at least none that I could see – I wondered if God was listening to me. Of course He was, but His responses to my pleas were not as *dramatic* as I wanted them to be, and they came in a way that I never suspected.

It was about that time that God brought L.C. Utley into my life. I listened to Brother Utley preach off and on for about ten years – from the time I was about six until I was sixteen. He taught me the Bible, and to lead singing. He also taught me something intangible – he taught me a side of God that I had not learned elsewhere – the gentle, kind, loving side of God. In some of the churches I attended as a young man, I learned the "facts" about God – and that is important – but L.C. Utley helped me to

experience God,

and he created a hunger in me for Godliness. He made me long for God as the deer pants for the water. I know now that L.C. Utley was God's initial answer to my prayers for holiness.

L.C. Utley left a mark on me that time will never erase. This next story is just one demonstration of how he did that.

Brother Utley told us that if we followed
every footprint that Jesus ever made,
there would not be a single one
that He would be ashamed of or
embarrassed by, and he hoped that when
we got older, that could be said for us.

6
L.C. Utley

When I search carefully through my "church memory," I have no recollections of a preacher earlier than L.C. Utley. I know that the "C" stood for Clyde, but I have no idea what the "L" stood for – or if it stood for anything. It seems that calling someone by their initials was quite common in those days – I remember other preachers named R.C. Oliver; B.C. Goodpasture; G.C. Brewer; H.A. Dixon; G.K. Wallace; N.B. Hardeman; and W.A. Bradfield.

I know there was an earlier preacher – one who preached at the Ferndale Church of Christ where my parents attended when I was a baby, because I heard my parents and others talk about him. I even know that his name was T.C. Willcox, and for some reason that completely baffles me, I know that the "T" stood for "Tip." I have no memory of his face, or ever hearing him preach.

Eventually, my parents, and a few other families left the Ferndale church, because it was so far from where we lived, and they formed a "church" of their own that met in various locations in Hazel Park. The first location I remember was an old school building. There couldn't have been more than twenty of us at first, but the number seemed to grow steadily. At some point, Brother Utley became our preacher. I have no memory of a specific sermon that he preached, and my impression, after all these years, is that he may not have been a particularly imposing or talented speaker. What impressed me deeply was his gentleness – his kindly, loving, soft-spoken, but fervent delivery.

Brother Utley's face is indelibly etched into my mind, as are his voice and his mannerisms. I think now, that God *providentially* brought L.C. Utley into my church life in the same way that He brought my first public school teacher, Miss Smokey, into my educational life. Just as Miss Smokey entered my life at that critical moment when my first and most lasting impressions of school were forming – so brother Utley entered my life when my first and most enduring impressions of church and preachers were forming.

My parents took me to many "gospel meetings" to hear famous preachers. For the most part, they seemed angry to me, and sometimes they frightened me. They spoke so loudly, and they pounded the pulpit – some marched arrogantly up and down the aisles, waving their arms and shouting at the top of their lungs – as they disclaimed vigorously about the implicit evils of dancing, moving picture shows, pool halls, alcohol, and other religions. They always closed their sermons with a vivid, Technicolor portrait of hell and its horrors and torments. They talked about it so realistically, that I sometimes wondered –

if they had been there

and even though I had never been to a dance, never seen a movie, or had a drink of the "devil's brew" – I was terrified!

Brother Utley wasn't like them at all. He never shouted, and although I'm sure he talked to us about hell, he made me believe that God didn't want me to go there – which was very reassuring. Every time he saw me he would say, "Why hello there Johnny." He had the most pleasant way of saying my name and placing his hand on my head – like he was pronouncing a blessing on me. He made me feel very special.

Every Sunday, between Sunday school and the worship service, Brother Utley would have all the kids come down front and sit on the front row. For about ten minutes he would teach us Bible facts and tell us Bible stories. Then the next week he would ask us questions about what he had taught us the week before. After the "lesson," the boys would stand up, and Brother Utley would start a song and we would pretend that we were leading the congregation. It always made me quite proud to "lead singing" for the whole church, and I can still see the look of pleasure on my mother's face.

The song I remember singing the most was, "Footprints of Jesus." After all these years – over fifty of them – I can still sing the words to all four verses without a book.

1. Sweetly Lord have we heard thee calling, come follow me.
   And we see where thy footprints falling, lead us to thee.

2. If they lead o'er the cold dark mountains, seeking his sheep,
   O'er along by Siloam's fountains, helping the weak.

3. If they lead through the temple holy, preaching the word;
   Or in homes of the poor and lowly serving the Lord.

4. By and by through the shining portals, turning our feet, we
   shall walk with the glad immortals, heavn's golden street.

Chorus: Footprints of Jesus, that make the pathway glow; We will follow the steps of Jesus, wher-e'er they go.

He would always find me after services and compliment me on what a "fine job" I had done, and tell me that some day he hoped I would "make a preacher."

After we sang the song, Brother Utley would talk to us about following in Jesus' footsteps. He said that actually it wasn't the "pathway" that glowed – it was Jesus' footprints that left sort of an iridescent reminder of His passing everywhere He went. He said that if we looked hard enough, we could see those footprints, and he told us that the Bible was sort of like a roadmap of the footprints of Jesus, and if we studied it, we would always be able to follow Him so we would know where to go. Brother Utley told us that if we followed every footprint that Jesus ever made, there would not be a single one that He would be ashamed of or embarrassed by, and he hoped that when we got older, that could be said for us.

He spoke so simply and convincingly that it never occurred to me that he was speaking *figuratively*, and I confess that I often looked in the dust of the road in front of my house, and on the way to school for Jesus' footprints. And sometimes, when I saw a clear set of them, I would follow them – looking for Jesus – until they faded or disappeared, and although I never exactly found Him – I certainly became a better boy because I looked.

I remember that one Saturday night it snowed heavily, and Sunday morning it was still snowing when we got to church. After Sunday school, Brother Utley had us boys up front leading singing, and after we sang "Footprints of Jesus," he said, "Boys, I want you to come with me," and he led us over to the window. When we got there he told us to look at the parking lot and tell him what we saw. We couldn't figure out what he wanted – and we gave some obvious answers like – the cars and the snow. Finally, he pointed to all of the footprints that people had left as they walked from their cars to the school building. He told us that everywhere we went we left footprints – whether we could see them or not – so it was important to be careful where we went.

I never forgot that lesson, and years later, sometimes when I went places that I should not have gone, when I left I would remember those footprints in the snow, and I would think about "Footprints of Jesus." I would see Brother Utley's face, and hear his kind, gentle voice, and I would be convicted and ashamed – and I often wished that I could go back and wipe out those footprints I had left behind me.

Yes, God used L.C. Utley as His "angel" – His "ministering servant" to answer my prayers by constantly calling me back to my dream of holiness. L.C. Utley taught me to *look* for God, and to *see* God, and to *believe* in God.

She said that an imagination was a wonderful thing, and she had often wondered the same things and she encouraged me to keep "imagining." If it hadn't been for Miss Smoky, I think I would have hated and resented school for the rest of my life.

7

Miss Smokey

This story is about another "angel" in my life. I have already mentioned her, but now I want to "introduce" her to you. I need also to tell you that she was not the answer to any specific prayer that I ever prayed. So, I never thought of her as an angel until I was much older and began not only to understand, but to appreciate the providential workings of God. Some of the "angels" He sends we don't even ask for, in fact, He sends angels when we don't even know enough to believe that there are angels.

Do you ever think about things that "might" happen to you in the future – all of the potential problems, both spiritual and physical, you are going to incur – and don't you wish that somehow you could either avoid, or at least "prepare" for those things? Now, think about yourself as a parent. As a parent you know that your children are going to have problems – they are going to have to make difficult decisions and there is no way you or they can avoid them – so all you can do is try to "prepare them." And that's what parents spend their lives doing – preparing their children for life – for all of the disappointments and struggles they will face.

Although we don't know the "specifics" of our children's problems – by specifics I mean the times, places, and circumstances under which those problems will come – we know the "types" of problems they will face, and so we often "anticipate" our children's needs. And what do we do when we anticipate the problems our children are going to have? We start taking specific steps to insure that they are prepared for those problems – Right? Of course right. How many parents and grandparents have a "college fund" – a fund that was started when your children were born, or even before – a fund your children know little if anything about – and in most cases – care nothing about. Why do we teach them manners, faith, sharing, thrift, self-discipline, honesty, a work ethic – because we know they are going to need those things in the future.

Now here's what I want you to think about: if you and I, with our limited vision, have the wisdom to "foresee," and the love to "plan," so that our children's future needs can be met – just think how our heavenly Father – with His infinite wisdom, foresight, love, and power – can act "providentially" to prepare us for what lies ahead.

This story illustrates how God in His gracious providence, often works for good in our lives without our knowledge or asking, by sending "angels" to accomplish His purposes. It also demonstrates how God can work through people even in "secular" settings to teach us "spiritual" lessons and prepare us for future service.

Jesus said in John 17:3, "Now this is eternal life: that they may know you, the only true God, and Jesus Christ whom you have sent." I believe that is the reason we are on this earth – to "know God." I believe that is the reason He created us "in His image" – so we would have the "ability" to know Him. If we don't learn anything else from the universe that He created, we learn that God has an incredible "imagination." And being created "in His image" means that we have an imagination also. Imagination, is a beautiful gift from God – and like all of God's gifts – it was given to us with a specific purpose in mind, because God will never be "known" only through the physical and rational senses. Without imagination, most of the spiritual and emotional aspects of our relationship with Him would be nonsense to us.

Those of you who have read my other books know that I have been "blessed" with a vivid imagination. I never did anything to "deserve" it – I was "born" with it. In that respect, I am no different from most children. A child's imagination is a fragile thing and, like all genetic gifts, it can be nurtured, and encouraged, or it can be poisoned and discouraged. I believe that the reason my imagination flowered and grew was "providential" – that God specifically prepared and brought people into my life at critical moments, so that His purposes "could be" fulfilled. (Please note "could be." God only creates "possibilities" for our lives – He does not "predetermine our responses" to those possibilities.)

I began my "formal education" in 1942, at a three-room, eight-grade school called Colerain. It was located on the corner of Eighteen Mile Road and John R, in Troy Township, Michigan. My school had eighteen-foot ceilings, and huge windows – it also had a "cloakroom" – a place where we left our lunches, hung our coats and hats, and left our boots. It was also the place where we went when we needed discipline, or when corporal punishment was applied. At Colerain School there was no office, no library, no principal, no gym, no cafeteria – and no nonsense.

My first teacher was Miss Smokey. Miss Smokey taught first, second, and third grade in the same room. I have no idea how she did that – but she not only did it – she did it extremely well. I believe that God "providentially" brought Miss Smokey into my life at that critical moment when my first impression of education was being formed. If some of my later teachers had been my first, my attitude toward school might have been totally different. Miss Smokey made me *want* to go to school – she made me believe that learning was the most exciting, important, wonderful thing in the world. She opened my mind to a whole new world – a world of books and ideas.

Miss Smokey encouraged my imagination because she had one of her own. I was a daydreamer. I didn't mean to daydream. It was just that I would hear something, or I would read something that caused my mind to wander, and I would start looking out those huge windows – and I would just gradually drift away. My next awareness would be Miss Smokey's hand gently shaking my shoulder – Miss Smokey had beautiful hands, with long, slender, graceful fingers – and from wherever I was – I would slowly begin to be aware that someone was calling my name –

"John? John?" She would say. And when I would finally awaken from my other world and look up at her, she would say,

"Where have you been John? Where have you been? How I wish I could have gone with you. Tell us what you see out that window." And she wasn't just patronizing me –

she really wanted to know.

And I would say, "Well, the first thing I saw was a robin, and I know that all robins look a lot alike, but sometimes you can tell the difference too. This one looked just like one I saw over by the creek on Sylvan Glenn Golf Course last Saturday, and I wondered if it was the same one. And then I got to thinking about the creek, and I wondered where the water comes from, and thinking about the water made me wonder if the water moves, or does it just tumble all over itself and stay in the same place? I wondered if the water I saw last Saturday was the same water I saw a week ago?"

And Miss Smokey didn't tell me to sit up and pay attention, and stop wondering about dumb things that don't amount to anything – she didn't tell me I was just willful, and didn't have any sense – like some of my later teachers. She said that an imagination was a wonderful thing, and she had often wondered the same things and she encouraged me to keep "imagining." If it hadn't been for Miss Smoky, I think I would have hated and resented school for the rest of my life. By the time I left Miss Smoky, and entered the fourth grade, I was so hooked on school that no one could take away the joy of reading or my determination to learn –

although there were those who tried.

Now that you have "met" Miss Smokey, I want to tell you a story about an incident that happened at Colerain School that had a long-term spiritual impact on my life.

I decided that if Miss Smokey thought Ansel
was okay, then he was okay with me too.
And if Miss Smokey thought that being like Jesus
was that important – I had better start learning
what He was like, so I could be more like Him.
I am glad to say that because of Miss Smokey,
I became Ansel's only other friend and defender,
I even went to his house and ate lunch with him.

8

Ansel Berkendorf

Ansel Berkendorf came to Colerain School in February 1944. His mother marched him into our classroom, completely unannounced one very cold, overcast morning, and placed him before Miss Smokey. Ansel's mother was a portly, red-faced woman, dressed in an ankle-length, nondescript dress, a huge, thick, black sweater that went almost to her knees, and she was wearing a babushka. You don't know the word "babushka?" My goodness, what do they teach in school these days? We have deleted "babushka," from our vocabulary and added "Internet" – it was a sorry exchange. A babushka is like a headscarf that ties under your chin. She would have made a classic portrait of a seventeenth-century peasant woman. Our school was populated mainly by lower middle-class students, who consequently dressed very modestly. By comparison, Russell and his mother were dressed in rags – and peculiar rags at that.

Ansel's mother spoke almost no English. I understood only the word "school," and the name "Ansel." I don't think that Miss Smokey understood Ansel's mother any better than I did, but she was simply magnificent. She smiled and made her feel welcome, and she acted like she understood every word Mrs. Berkendorf said. She assured her that she was happy to have Ansel, and that she would help him in every way she could.

Ansel didn't want to stay. He was obviously terrified. He cried and clung tenaciously to his mother. After communicating her desire to place Ansel in our school, his mother turned and placed both of her hands on Ansel's shoulders. I wish I could draw you a picture of that scene. It must have made a heavy impression upon me, because I can see them so clearly now; her round, rough, red face, worn by cares, old far before its time; her stubby, callused, work-hardened fingers with the black dirt visible under the broken nails; her short, square body trembling –

she addressed him in German.

I will never know what she said, but Ansel stopped crying, squared his shoulders and accepted his fate. Finally they separated, and Miss Smokey took Ansel by the hand, and led him to an unoccupied desk in the third grade row. She immediately supplied him with pencil and paper – explained that we no longer used the "ink well" on his desk – and what the school routines were. He sat all day in absolute silence, never acknowledging our stares or even our presence. He did not go out for recess, or for lunch.

You must understand that it was 1944. Our country was engaged in a bitter conflict with Germany. The Germans were our enemies. Even as children we had learned to hate, and there is no discrimination in a child's hatred. Ansel was German. He had a German name, he wore German clothes, he spoke with a German accent, and we hated him. Children can be absolutely brutal. We never accepted Ansel. He was never spoken to in a friendly way – he was never asked to play a game or chosen for a team, he was taunted, heckled, called "Kraut," and "Nazi" – we would imitate a German salute and say "Heil, Hitler" – he was abused in every way –

and he was alone.

He gradually – painfully worked his way into the school routines, but he was a person apart. He had not a single friend, except Miss Smokey. Miss Smokey was kind to Ansel – she made him think he was special by staying after school with him. She brought him clothes – she supplied him with books, paper, and pencils out of her own pocket. Her Herculean efforts to teach him, to reach him, to help him with his clothes, his speech – and when Ansel was absent, to blast us with her speeches for our cruelty – are an everlasting monument to her and to her kind. I thank God for Miss Smokey – Ansel's only friend.

Ansel's life with us reached a climax late that spring. As you can easily imagine, he was a poor student. He barely spoke English. He never had paper or pencil, but always suffered the humiliation of having to *borrow* from Miss Smokey. He would not ask of us –

he knew the answer.

One bright, warm spring day Miss Smokey, in an attempt to rouse the interest of her flagging students, promised an afternoon holiday to our class if everyone scored a hundred on a spelling test. She obviously forgot about Ansel. It wasn't a very hard test – even Ansel might have passed it – but he didn't. Whether he was paying us back, or whether he just didn't know, I can't guess. We graded each other's papers, and then read the scores out loud. Sure enough, Ansel was the only one who missed a word – and we missed our holiday.

Now I come to the worst part of this story. After school, two other boys and I jumped Ansel and roughed him up. I don't know what good we thought it would do. Even after fifty years the ache in my heart is almost unbearable.

Miss Smokey found out what we had done. She took me into the cloakroom separately from the other two boys. She was furious – I had never seen her so angry. She told me that she had never been so disappointed in a person in her life – she said that she expected more from me than that. She asked me how I could do such a thing – and when I said that I didn't know, she said, "Don't you go to church?" And when I said that I went all the time she said,

> "Well, it doesn't seem to have done you much good.
> What do they teach you at that church?
> Whatever it is, it hasn't helped you to be like Jesus."

That really hurt – and it made me think too.

Miss Smokey made me feel like I was about the sorriest person she had ever met. She changed my mind about Ansel Berkendorf – and about Germans – and about anybody who was different – and she helped me to understand that people aren't bad because of where they're born, or who their parents are – that I had to learn to look deeper than that.

Miss Smokey made me see myself as a very small person, and she made me see Ansel as more than a German. I decided that if Miss Smokey thought Ansel was okay, then he was okay with me too. And if Miss Smokey thought that being like Jesus was that important – I had better start learning what He was like, so I could be more like Him. I am glad to say that because of Miss Smokey, I became Ansel's only other friend and defender, I even went to his house and ate lunch with him. I'm also glad to say that I started taking my Christianity a lot more seriously and practically.

God used Miss Smokey as one of His "angels" to teach me a critically important lesson about people – a lesson I ought to have learned at home or at church – but didn't. It was a lesson I needed to learn, a lesson that was vital to the ministry I would enter years later; and so God used His "angel," Miss Smokey to teach it to me. I never forgot that lesson, and I hope that you never do.

Maybe we ought to be asking ourselves if going to church "does us much good" – and maybe we ought to be checking into what we "teach" in our churches – and if it helps us to

be like Jesus.

I certainly didn't think of it at the time —
but it occurs to me now that maybe God
used me as "someone else's angel" that night.
Maybe another weary pilgrim, searching for a
place to stand, would travel that road that night —
or in the days to come — and see that sign
and take heart. Remember that God is not
only trying constantly to reveal Himself to you —
He is using you to reveal Himself to others —
you may be His providential "angel."

Jesus Cares

As a person of faith, you must believe that God cares about you – about your struggles, pain, loneliness, depression, and heartache. God cares when you are worried about your children, your job, your marriage, and your health. He is constantly trying to reassure us – to touch us in a way that will bring us comfort and hope.

One of the ways that He does that is by sending His "angels" to us at those moments when we are most sensitive to Him – when our hearts are broken – when we are in despair – when we are truly "looking" for Him, Remember that it is specifically those who are "weary and heavy laden" that Jesus calls to Himself. I don't suppose that's the way He wants it – He would just as soon call those who are happy and carefree – but we are all aware that most often it is our sorrows that bring us to our knees and make us aware of our need for Him. Sometimes he reminds us of His love in the most unusual ways – in ways that under "normal" circumstances we would never see Him. This next story is about one of those times.

I was returning from speaking at a lectureship in a small West Texas town. It was late at night; I was very tired. I was driving alone across what appears to be endless flatness. I was depressed. I felt – I think, *inadequate* is the right word. Do you ever feel inadequate? Things were just piling up. The congregation I was preaching for was deeply involved in two theological and emotional "issues" that had far-reaching implications, threatening its unity and spiritual health, and I was at odds with the leadership as to how to resolve them.

I was also involved in several marriage and personal counseling situations that were impossible for me to, "leave at the office." The people who had come to me for counseling were drowning in a sea of insensitivity, immoral conduct, miscommunication and selfishness, and I felt responsible for "fixing them." Part of the problem was that I had no "power" to determine the outcome. By "power" I mean that I could not "control" their actions. All I had was my words and my prayers, and I felt terribly "inadequate." Both of these situations were taking a heavy toll on my own mental and spiritual health.

Feeling inadequate was not new to me, neither was it inappropriate.

I am inadequate – terribly so,

and I am not in control.

But even within the boundaries of that realization I had come to expect, and others certainly expected that I could "do" something to "make it better."

Usually, at this stage of depression, some survival mechanism flips the little switch in my brain which in turn lights up a mental monitor that has a red-lettered, digital display which reads, "count your blessings" – and that is exactly what happened. Truthfully, all that did was to "tick me off" – because at that moment I was not interested in counting my blessings. It's not that I don't have them, it's just that no matter what level of blessing I have, it only serves as the foundation from which I attempt to leap to the next level.

When people – who perceive themselves as having fewer blessings than I – tell me, with some degree of recrimination, to "count my blessings," what they mean is that they have already counted them – and although *they* have room to complain, *I* do not. When people who have more blessings than I do tell me – with a note of condescension – to "count my blessings" – they only mean that I should be content with less than they have. And so at every level we see that *blessings* are those things which others have. What I have are either what I *deserve* or the *necessities*, and nobody counts necessities or is grateful for them.

By the time I had worked my way through that mental muddle, I had covered about thirty miles. I paused in my deliberations long enough to check my rearview mirror, to turn up the beeper on my radar detector, and to look about me. No perceivable change in the landscape was apparent, and so I lapsed back into the depression that had darkened my thoughts.

The miles crawled by endlessly. Just before I got to Odonell, I tried the radio for a diversion, some song about old dogs, children, and watermelon wine being the only things in the world worth a dime, came wailing at my injured ears – greater depression. I tried listening to the tape of my lecture – massive trauma.

It was dark, there was no traffic, and truthfully I hadn't been paying too much attention to my driving, but as I rounded a slight curve, and my headlights swept the roadside, I noticed a piece of paper fluttering in the wind. It was loosely attached to an old mesquite fence post, and just as my headlights swept by it, it turned and revealed its message. The sign was old, faded, and hanging precariously, and although I couldn't make out all of the letters, I knew what it said:

"JES
CAR"

I had driven down this road many times, and of course I had passed it before – several times – but I had never "seen it." Some pilgrim had taken the time and gone to the trouble to post this poignant reminder, and tonight, of all the dark nights in the year,

I had seen it.

Why tonight? Why just now? Why at this exact, precise moment? If that sign had turned three seconds earlier or later, I would not have seen the message. If it had been daylight, or if it had been under different circumstances, I would have paid no attention. Could it be that God had sent an angel to turn the sign just as I passed, so that my headlights would reflect off of it? Could it be that because of my frame of mind I was "tuned" to receive just such a message? Oh I pray to God that it was so – and I pray to God that you will believe that He is constantly trying to help you to see that message on your dark days.

I hit the brakes, made a "U" turn and went back. I parked my car where my headlights would light the area, and made my way, suit, white shirt, tie, dress shoes and all, through the bar ditch, to the old fence. I straightened the sign, secured it as best I could with some baling wire, and went back to the car feeling that I was not quite as useless as I had imagined – and knowing that –

I was in control of some things.

I went on up the highway a short distance, made another "U" turn and drove slowly back by the sign – "my sign." I could see it plainly now, and so could any other sojourner traveling this way.

"JESUS
CARES!"

He really does you know, and sometimes,
when we really need it, His caring makes
all the difference.

I certainly didn't think of it at the time – but it occurs to me now that maybe God used me as "someone else's angel" that night. Maybe another weary pilgrim, searching for a place to stand, would travel that road that night – or in the days to come – and see that sign and take heart. Remember that God is not only trying constantly to reveal

Himself to you – He is using you to reveal Himself to others – you may be His providential "angel."

As I was writing this, the words to one of our great hymns came to my mind.

> "God moves in a mysterious way,
> His wonders to perform.
> He plants His footsteps in the sea,
> And rides upon the storm."

It is not angels He wants you to believe in –
angels can't save you – they are simply God's
wonderful messengers. Their job is not to
attract you to them – but to attract you to God –
to point you to the gospel and the atoning work
of Jesus. But the gospel isn't just anywhere –
it is in the Bible – and the Bible is God's revelation
of Himself – and unless you find God
in the Bible – you will never find Him at all.

10
He Is There

The following story is a painful one for me. Writing about it brings it all back – makes it seem like yesterday – it opens the old wounds and the old hurt. Darkness, and bewilderment springs back to life again as I relive the incident by writing it down. But by the grace of God, the story also brings back the hope, and the reassuring light that shone on my life because of the faith that the incident produced.

Luke 10:38-42 gives us one of those marvelous insights into the daily life of Jesus.

> As Jesus and his disciples were on their way, he came to a village where a woman named Martha opened her home to him. She had a sister called Mary, who sat at the Lord's feet listening to what he said. But Martha was distracted by all the preparations that had to be made. She came to him and asked, "Lord, don't you care that my sister has left me to do the work by myself? Tell her to help me!" "Martha, Martha," the Lord answered, "you are worried and upset about many things, but only one thing is needed. Mary has chosen what is better, and it will not be taken away from her."

What never ceases to amaze me – what is astonishing to me – is the ability of Jesus to take an incident so common – so trivial – so unspectacular – an incident that most people would have either totally ignored or simply passed it off as too routine to bother mentioning it. But Jesus sees in this moment an opportunity to turn it into a life – changing event that has been preserved for two thousand years, and has had a profound impact on millions of lives.

I believe I had an almost idyllic childhood. I had a great home – filled with singing, Bible reading, good food, laughter, and friends. My parents, who loved me fervently, were active, involved Christians, and consequently were home every night, and did not drink, swear, yell, or fight with each other. I had a sister, who was six years older than I, who was a great companion, teacher, and role model.

Although we were very poor, by today's standards, I had no awareness of it – or if I did – it made no impression on me because I had no materialistic ambitions. I only remember wanting three things during all of my early years: a Daisy, Red Rider BB gun, a Hillrich and Bradsby, Louisville Slugger baseball bat, and a "coaster" sled – all of which I got.

I lived in a rural setting, with room to roam and have a dog – my constant and faithful companion – Ginger. I had great friends, a great teacher at school, and the church we attended was filled with people my parents' age and consequently with children my age. We had the greatest time together – I loved going to church. I was an adventuresome child who feared nothing, and accordingly was constantly on the edge of disaster. However, I somehow believed that the entire world was a wonderful place, full of delightful people and enchanted forests, and I could not conceive that anyone or anything would ever try to harm me.

That romantic view of the world continued for what I believe was an abnormally long time – until I was in my mid-teens in fact. I do not mean that there weren't some occasional setbacks – no negative incidents or momentary clouds. Both of my grandmothers died, my uncle Ray died, Ginger died, there were problems at the church we attended. My family began to move a lot – my growing involvement in sports and with girls brought me occasional pain – things like that happened along the way, but they passed from my consciousness quickly, and I was able to shrug them off as merely temporary, unimportant, inexplicable incidents.

I began preaching at the age of nineteen, and I began to get serious with girls and cars at about the same time – which by the way – truthfully is a very bad combination. As a result, things began to happen – things that I couldn't shrug off. I began to be troubled by religious and moral questions that I couldn't resolve satisfactorily. I started not being able to go to sleep for the first time in my life. I began to lose interest in the things that had always brought me pleasure; and my religious and prayer life began to take on more serious and complicated tones. My beautiful, simple, romantic, idyllic, childhood world ended in pain and confusion.

I have given you this brief sketch of my early life in order to give you a context for the story I want to share with you. I also assume that each of you went through, are going through, or will go through, something similar. If you don't understand this background, you wouldn't understand the story.

A series of disastrous events in my late teens and early twenties brought about my first experience with depression. A combination of finding myself at odds with some traditional understandings of Scripture; unable to harmonize the realities of life with the unreality of many church traditions; the oppressing reality of sin in my life, not overt sin, as much as the depth of evil that I was capable of conceiving; my inability to deal with it or find cleansing – left me lonely and terribly depressed. I did not call it that – I just knew that I felt lousy all the time. I went from finding joy and purpose in almost everything, to not being able to find it in anything.

I tried to talk to my parents about it – but I found their responses totally unsatisfying. I tried to talk to my friends, but their solutions were contrary to my moral principles – actually, they were as lost as I was – only they didn't know it. I tried to find peace in a relationship with a girl – but that proved to be a disaster. I tried working harder at my preaching ministry, I gave myself to sports and to fast cars – but nothing filled the emptiness – the lostness inside of me. My parents, my friends, my girl, work, sports, cars – none of them could "save me." In despair I left home – everything that was familiar – I quit my job, sold my meager possessions – and hitched a ride to Los Angeles – looking for something I could not have identified to save my life.

I soon ran out of money, I was friendless and broke, and I began sleeping on beaches, park benches, and at Salvation Army centers. I finally got a job doing clean-up work at a mobile home factory – working with people who couldn't speak English. I got a room at the Lomita Hotel – a shabby, disreputable, run-down place that was home to about twenty longshoremen who were absolutely the roughest, crudest, most vulgar, profane, immoral people I had ever met. I walked to work, and I walked – I started to say "home" – but no place I ever lived was further from "home" than the Lomita Hotel.

I had to work a week before I got paid, so I sold two or three articles of clothing I had for food money, but it didn't last. I found myself with four days to go until payday, and no money. I thought I would just "fast" for four days, and I did okay the first day, but it was hot at work and my job demanded maximum physical exertion. After the second day, I was weak and a little dizzy. The third day I was desperate. That night I borrowed a dollar from one of the longshoremen, and that night I went to the owner-operated diner just down the street. I sat on a stool at the counter.

Even in those days, a dollar didn't buy much. I went over the menu meticulously, trying to get the most for my dollar. I ordered a "pork dinner," and when it came I tried to eat slowly – savoring each bite – but it didn't last long.

While I was eating, I began to think about my mother's cooking

– and I thought about home – church potlucks, singings, my friends, and what I used to be. The full realization of my lostness and sinfulness settled over me. I saw clearly how far I had fallen, and what I had become. A blanket of black depression, regret, and guilt settled over me such as I had never experienced. I rested my head on my arms, which were placed on the counter, and I cried.

I had scarcely noticed that a man had come in and occupied the stool next to me. I became aware of him, when he turned and tried to console me in an almost unintelligible way. He was obviously very drunk. He had ordered the largest steak dinner on the menu, and it was served to him just as I raised my head. He looked at it – shoved it across the counter – stated emphatically that he didn't want it – paid for it and left.

The owner-cook must have sensed my desperate condition as I stared unbelievingly at the forsaken plate. "You want this buddy?" he said.

It was delicious.

Under other circumstances, it would seem a small and insignificant gesture, something so incidental that it would be quickly forgotten, certainly not worth writing down . . . but to a lost and wandering child, seeking a place to stand, a reason to be . . . it was a spectacular ray of light that pierced the darkness in my soul. It was a friendly hand on my shoulder, a reassuring voice calling my name out of the darkness.

"John. Son, I'm still here.
Don't lose heart. I'm watching, I'm concerned –
I'll see you through this."

This was the critical event – the turning point in my restoration. When I got back to my room, I fell on my knees beside my bed and thanked God for His providential reassurance. I honestly didn't think of this at that time – but could it be that this "drunk" was an "angel" of God? Could it be that God in His infinite wisdom and mysterious way of working His will decided to answer my prayers in this way?

You don't have to go to Los Angeles to find God – He is as close to you right now as He has ever been, and His "ministering spirits" are constantly looking for opportunities to remind us of His providential care.

What Jesus says to Martha's frustration is, "There is only one important thing – and that is knowing God." In the midst of your struggles – your loneliness, your disappointments, frustrations – your lostness – I hope you will remember that. Your parents can't save you. Your wife or husband can't save you. Your children and friends can't save you. Psychology and philosophy, drugs and pills can't save you. Work and sports and busyness and entertainment can't save you. Not even good works and the church can save you. If you want to be saved – you must believe that God wants to save you and that He is looking for those moments and those ways to reach out to you – to tell you that He cares and that you must trust Him. His angels are messengers sent to seize those precious moments when your heart is open to Him.

Everything God does is to help you to come to obedient faith. It is not angels He wants you to believe in – angels can't save you – they are simply God's wonderful messengers. Their job is not to attract you to them – but to attract you to God – to point you to the gospel and the atoning work of Jesus. But the gospel isn't just anywhere – it is in the Bible – and the Bible is God's revelation of Himself – and unless you find God in the Bible – you will never find Him at all.

Although God did not tell me to write what I saw

and send it to anybody, I thought I would anyway.

My prayer: that you will read and believe, and

that believing, God would be more able to bring

you the blessings that He has in store for you.

11
Mount Soledad and the Cross

One last story. I tell it for several reasons. First, I tell it because it happened fairly recently – during my adulthood – and I wanted you to know that neither my nor your "angel stories" are confined to childhood. Second, I tell it because it has to do with another aspect of "angels" – those who "speak" to us, but are not seen in any form. Another reason I tell it is because it has to do with "hope," and hope is the cornerstone of the Christian religion. Believing in Jesus allows us to live in hope in our darkest hours. In the movie, *Shawshank Redemption*, the main character says, "Hope is a good thing – maybe the best of things – and no good thing ever dies." It's true you know, hope is a good thing – maybe the best of things, and those who place all of their hopes in Jesus will never die. Hope is tied irretrievably to faith – faith that God does indeed love us, care about us, and is constantly working providentially to remind us of His involvement in our lives.

It is important to me that you know that I believe that the "messages" these angels bring to us are first, *only* for those to whom they speak and second, that they never "tell us" anything that contradicts or circumvents the revealed will of God in Scripture.

I got up early on the morning of March 3, 1999, to go and run at Mission Bay Park in San Diego, California. I left the house not long after daylight, drove to the park and began plodding my weary and disinterested way along the sidewalk. I don't enjoy running—not at all, it is an act of mental, spiritual, and physical discipline for me. Because I don't enjoy running - actually, what I do should not be called "running," anyone who saw me would not say, "Oh look, there's a man running." They would probably say, "What is that man doing, maybe we ought to stop and see if he needs help?"

I'm not sure that what I do even qualifies for "jogging" but that is closer to what I do – anyway – because I jog very slowly, I keep my head down and watch my feet and the sidewalk. Watching the sidewalk gives me a much greater sense of speed and distance than looking ahead. If I look ahead, my progress is so imperceptible that I have to look at my feet to make sure that I'm actually moving.

The bad thing about watching the sidewalk and my feet, is that I miss a lot. This morning I started out running north. It had been very foggy the night before, and I noticed when I got our of the car that the whole area of Pacific Beach was blanketed in a vague, shifting, gradually undulating blanket of gray-white mist. It gave the impression of a vast, distant, unending, and mysterious ocean made of pie dough. The fog was so thick, that if a person had not seen the area before, they might have thought that it hid an impenetrable forest.

From where I was, it was as though Pacific Beach had disappeared – actually it was more like it had never been—and I felt as though I was running toward something rather frightening and sinister – something unknown and threatening. It gave me the shivers, and I tried even harder to keep my eyes on the pavement just ahead.

Things went well for perhaps half a mile, but I started hearing this "voice" that urged me to look up. At first, the "voice" was soft and indistinct, and I had no trouble resisting it – but finally – it increased its volume to a shout – and although I would not say it was audible to any ears but mine – it certainly could no longer be ignored – "Look up" it said insistently! And almost unwillingly – I yielded and looked up.

The same uneasy, nebulous, lumpy landscape greeted my glance, and since I was closer, it seemed even more ominous in its impenetrable vagueness. I was about to return to staring at my feet when the voice said, "Look further up you idiot" this was said with some degree of impatience, and I looked around to make sure I was alone. Seeing no one, I raised my eyes even further, hoping to find some reason for looking up, something solid, something to point to—something to at least satisfy the insistent voice. And there, rising above the towering banks of fog, was the very top of Mount Soledad – with the brilliant sun shining on the white buildings that are there, and above those buildings, at the very top, those glorious sun rays were glistening and reflecting from the cross that towers above the mountain. It was as though I was seeing across time – or beyond it, and I stopped and marveled.

As I stood there in absolute awe, I thought of the people in Pacific Beach who were living in that fog, and I thought that if I went to them and told them that just a short distance away the sun was shining on the mountain, they probably wouldn't believe me, because when you live in the fog – it's hard to believe in the mountain, or the sun, or the cross – because the fog seems endless and it destroys hope.

It also occurred to me that the selfishness, lust, and materialism that had dominated my thinking most of my life – had caused me to see, as Paul said, "through a glass darkly" – but all my life I had, by the grace of God, hoped that the mountain with the cross was there – and all my life I knew that I had to go through the fog if I was ever going to reach the mountain and the cross. But sometimes, the fog was so thick that I lost my way, and my faith in the mountain and the cross wavered.

Today, I felt as though God had lifted the fog of my life for just a moment, and allowed me to actually see the mountain and the cross—so that my hope might be renewed. I would have missed it if he had not sent his angel to tell me to, "Look up," so that I could be reassured that it was indeed there. I thought about how God had allowed John the Revelator to see into heaven, and then sent his angel to tell him to, "Write on a scroll what you see and send it to the seven churches." He urged John to "write" so that you and I might have the hope – "blessed assurance" that heaven is indeed there – as certain as hope itself, solid, real, tangible – and to make us confident that our hope is not a foolish and childish fancy – there is an end to uncertainty, there is life beyond the grave

On the way home I thought of those who wish to remove the cross from Mt Soledad for reasons that are unintelligible to me. And I wondered why in a world so filled with fog – with uncertainty, doubt, so crushed with hatred, poverty, sin, and pain and hopelessness – why would anyone want to destroy the one thing that has brought more solid hope to the world than any other single thing.

We must never confuse hope with "wishing" – hope has substance, foundation—where wishing has none. Our hope has foundation—because our hope is ultimately not in this world – it is in the resurrection of Jesus Christ and His promise that He would return for us.

Although God did not tell me to write what I saw and send it to anybody, I thought I would anyway, and I pray that you will read and believe, and that believing, your hope might be renewed, and God would send His angel to remind you that –

"Hope is a good thing,
Maybe the best of things,
And no good thing ever dies."

"Oh what peace we often forfeit,

Oh what needless pain we bear,

all because we do not carry,

everything to God in prayer."

I believe that verse speaks a great truth.

Why do we not carry everything to God in prayer?

I think the answer is that when it comes right down

to it – we don't believe in supernatural intervention

and divine providence – and we certainly

don't believe in angels. We don't "carry everything

to God in prayer" because we don't believe that He

has any practical way of responding to our pleas.

12

"What a Friend We Have in Jesus"

Because I grew up in a singing family and a singing church, the songs of Zion have made a more lasting impression on me than the sermons I have heard. One reason for this is that I believe my a cappella heritage caused songs and their messages to be more deeply ingrained into my theology. Truthfully, I am fully convinced that we often sang a better theology than we preached.

One of my favorite songs is that great old hymn, "What a Friend We Have in Jesus." For some reason, that song has impacted my spiritual thinking since I was a child. I believe that one of the reasons for this is that in the church I grew up in – the sermons I heard did not lead me to think of Jesus as my "friend," and I believe it was a great consolation to me to think of Him in that way. One of the verses says, "Oh what peace we often forfeit, Oh what needless pain we bear, all because we do not carry, everything to God in prayer."

I believe that verse speaks a great truth. Why do we not carry everything to God in prayer? I think the answer is that when it comes right down to it – we don't believe in supernatural intervention and divine providence – and we certainly don't believe in angels. We don't "carry everything to God in prayer" because we don't believe that He has any practical way of responding to our pleas. I am reminded of the story in Mark 9:17-32 of the man who brought his demon possessed son to the disciples in the hope that they could cure him and when they failed, Jesus says, in verse nineteen,

"Bring the boy to me." When the boy is brought to Jesus, he immediately falls down in a convulsive seizure – and the father says to Jesus,

"*If* you can do anything, take pity on us and help us." Jesus says,

"*If* you can?" and I think the context demands that we read – "How dare you say – '*If* you can'? To say 'if' to Me is an insult and indignity that is almost impossible to bear. 'If,' you say – let Me tell you that I could make your son stronger than Hercules and swifter than Apollo – I could make him the next Roman emperor – and all you want Me to do is cast out this demon?"

Many of us have been raised in a spiritual culture that has tended to deny the miraculous – probably because of our utilitarian and pragmatic approach to Scripture and life. We would "prefer" to believe that God no longer works "in mysterious ways" because that would destroy the syllogistic approach we have taken to our theology.

I might add that this same type of thinking prevails in our "dot com" world. Many people reject the gospel outright because it "makes no sense" – by which they mean that they are uncomfortable with anything that can't be performed by either mental or physical exercise or programmed into a computer.

I have counseled with many people who had no "peace" in their lives – and they came to me, thinking that I could give them words and suggestions that would somehow empower them to perform deeds that would eliminate the pain and depression that had settled over them. And when I told them what I had to offer them was Jesus and the gospel – they laughed derisively and said – "I don't think you understand, I need some 'real help, not hocus – pocus'." And like the rich ruler – they went away sorrowfully – forfeiting the only "real peace" there is – and bearing their pain needlessly. The question is never "if" God can – it is a question of our faith in His love for us and our willingness to accept His intervention.

The conversation between this father and Jesus ends in a way that ought to be echoed by all of us: When Jesus says, "Everything is possible to him who believes" – the boy's father exclaims, "I *do* believe; help me overcome my unbelief!" Isn't that what we all need? Don't we all need God to help us overcome our unbelief? May God send His "ministering servants" to us and open our eyes to see His Son.

In Matthew 8, Matthew records an incident that reveals another common human failing. A man who has leprosy comes to Jesus with a request for healing, and he approaches Jesus in this way. "Lord, if you are *willing*, you can make me clean." This man doesn't question Jesus' "power" he questions His "willingness" – perhaps His "goodness." I think this man is more like most believers than the one mentioned above. We are quite willing to say, "Oh I know that God 'can' do anything" – because we know that is the "right thing" – the "politically correct" thing to say in religious discussion. But we always give God – and ourselves – a way out by adding this disclaimer – "of course if it is according to His will."

We must make very sure that the phrase we "tack on" to the end on our prayers – "if it be Your will" – is a statement of faith in God's supreme wisdom and not simply a statement of unbelief. The incident with the man with leprosy ends this way – "Jesus reached out his hand and touched the man. 'I am willing,' he said. 'Be clean!'" Immediately he was cured of his leprosy."

I tell you that the reason we have no cure for our "diseases" has nothing to do with either God's power or His willingness – it has to do with our faith. Our prayers are so small, trivial, and inconsequential that God must be constantly frustrated by them. I think God often says to me, "Is that all you want Me to do for you? Give you a safe journey, cure your cancer? My goodness, I can certainly do that and I will do that – but I could do so much more – I could open the heavens for you and let you see Jesus at My right hand if you had the courage to ask and the faith to receive."

I have told you all of these stories because
I thought you might enjoy them, learn from them,
be challenged by them – and blessed by them.
But equally important, I thought that you might
remember incidents and people from your own life –
and you might see in them the providential workings
of God and fall to your knees in gratitude.

Epilogue

Looking back after all these years, it occurs to me that children probably "see" many more angels than adults. I do not say that they "have" more angels in their lives – I only say that they "see" more. The only angel – in the sense of "heavenly beings" – I ever "saw" was the one in the first story I told. I have not "seen" one since. That does not at all mean that there have been no angels in my life since then – or that God only sends angels to children. It means that a child's faith is not hampered by a lack of imagination. It is not restricted by logic, facts, or previous experience. Lawyers, accountants, salesmen, technicians, physicists, philosophers, plumbers, principals, physicians, psychiatrists, preachers, electricians, and especially theologians basically cannot "see" angels at all. They are like those two men in Luke 24 who were walking home on the road from Jerusalem to Emmaus talking about Jesus and the crucifixion. When Jesus joined them – they didn't even recognize Him – because their imaginations had been systematically destroyed by the utilitarian legalism of their religion.

Perhaps this is why Jesus said that if we didn't become like little children we would never enter the kingdom of God. And although I don't believe that seeing angels is necessary to salvation, I do believe that those who see them pray better, see God more clearly, love God more dearly – are much more happy, contented, peaceful, and rewarded by their faith.

I have told you all of these stories because I thought you might enjoy them, learn from them, be challenged by them – and blessed by them. But equally important, I thought that you might remember incidents and people from your own life – and you might see in them the providential workings of God and fall to your knees in gratitude.

I also hoped that you might have more faith in angels, and even more importantly, that you might believe in them "practically" so that you would be more able to pray "in faith," with no doubts. That because you have a better understanding of "how" God answers our prayers – you might pray more. I wanted you to remember that you should not –

> "forget to entertain strangers,
> for by so doing some people
> have entertained angels without knowing it."
> HEBREWS 13:2